RETIREMENTQUEST

RETIREMENT *Quest*

Make Better Decisions

John Hauserman, CFP®

Retirement Journey, LLC • Towson, Maryland

RetirementQuest
Make Better Decisions
by John Hauserman, CFP®

Published by Retirement Journey, LLC
P.O. Box 626
Ellicott City, Maryland 21041
www.retirementquest.com
contact@retirementquest.com
877-233-4912

Examples offered in this book are hypothetical and for illustrative purposes only. They are not indicative of or guarantees of any investing result. There is a risk that not all investment objectives will be met.

Investors should carefully consider the investment objectives, risks, charges, and expenses of any investment company before investing. Prospectuses contain this and other information about investments, and they can be obtained from your financial representative. Read the prospectus carefully before investing or sending money.

RetirementQuest is a registered trademark of Retirement Journey, LLC.

ISBN: 978-0-9830217-0-4

Manufactured in the United States of America

Design and composition: www.dmargulis.com

To my wife, Diane, and children, Jackson and Leah, who mean more to me than all of the wealth in the world; to my clients whose faith I treasure; and to all the young people of the world who depend on us. I do this for you.

Contents

	Preface	IX
	Acknowledgments	XI
1	The Predicament of Life Expectancy	3
2	Goal Setting	6
3	Gather the Information	12
4	Crunch the Numbers	16
5	Adjustments	30
6	Risk Management	36
7	Risk in a Modern World	47
8	Investing	53
9	What about Cash, Bonds, and Stocks?	60
10	Investor Behavior	69
11	Choosing a Source of Advice	79
12	The Market Cycle	86
13	A Dark Pact on a Summer Day	99
14	The Boomers	103
15	Born into Peace and Prosperity	106
16	A Look Ahead	113
	Notes	122
	Index	125

Preface

TODAY'S RETIREE HOPEFULS find themselves perched precariously between the proverbial rock and hard place. On one hand, they are deeply concerned about funding their own impending retirement. Simultaneously, these children of the twentieth century are terrified about the third-world-like economic mess they are set to leave their progeny. Fortunately, our collective story does not have to end this way. The book you hold in your hands draws upon my two decades of financial planning experience and was written to help readers make better decisions. Additional resources which may prove helpful in your retirement quest include the RetirementQuest® interactive planning map and the RetirementQuest Tool Box, both of which can accessed at no cost from www.RetirementQuest.com.

Studies suggest most Americans are poor investors, typically failing to reach important goals or underperforming the various markets in which they are invested.[1] At the same time, employer-sponsored retirement plans are increasingly requiring participants to enter the often unforgiving world of stocks, bonds, and mutual funds. We live in a world of nonstop news and downloadable data. How do we sort through all this information to develop the knowledge we need to make better retirement planning decisions?

The journey toward solid decision making begins at, well, the beginning. Modern psychology tells us that most decisions are triggered by underlying emotions, which in turn are shaped by the experiences we have throughout our lives, especially those of our early years. Sound retirement planning rests on a foundation of basic financial knowledge. With this knowledge, you can set goals for your retirement years and take wise steps toward achieving them. You may not choose to become an investment aficionado, but you can be in a stronger position to either handle your own affairs or to evaluate the competency of the professionals you hire to assist you.

Although the common investor pitfalls covered in this book are not great in number, they do tend to recur with astonishing regularity. To avoid them, individuals must exercise extreme vigilance. Excellent financial planning should prepare individuals for the emotional as well as technical task at hand.

RetirementQuest does not simply rehash the familiar old investment axioms found in so many of today's volumes. Instead, it offers a holistic approach that explores the ways in which the financial services industry, politics, and modern media all too often combine to hamper rather than encourage our personal saving efforts. By improving our understanding of the overall process, we can avoid falling prey to these hazards and take steps to potentially provide for our own financial future and that of our children.

Acknowledgments

TO THE STAFF at Financial Council Incorporated, my partners in planning, I can't thank you enough for taking such good care of my clients. I'd also like to acknowledge the entire team at FCI for their expert financial counsel, camaraderie, and friendship. Additionally I would like to recognize the fine work of Dick Margulis and Susanna Sturgis without whom this book would have never come to fruition.

RETIREMENTQUEST

1

The Predicament
of Life Expectancy

I N 1935, WHEN the Social Security program came into being, the average male worker could expect to survive into his mid-sixties. Typically, the average male worker's spouse had a life span of a few additional years. College attendance was the exception, rather than the norm, so most entered the workforce in their middle to late teens. As a result, a hiree could expect to work for about 40 years and would not have to cover either college or nursing-home expenses. Instead, if an elderly parent needed care, the chore generally fell upon a stay-at-home spouse. The task of caring for an aged parent usually ended sometime during the peak earning years. When parents died, they often left behind a home unencumbered by debt, which could provide something of an inheritance for their offspring.

A career of 40-plus years followed by 6 to 10 years of retirement made funding a simpler task. As a hypothetical example, if a worker socked away just 5% of his income for that time period and earned a 6% investment return on his money, he would accumulate approximately 7 to 8 years' worth of salary. With the mortgage paid off and possibly a small inheritance, even modest spending discipline would prove sufficient.

When Social Security arrived, the assumed math became even easier. A disciplined savings regimen of approximately 3% of working income, compounded at a 6% rate of return or so, would generally suffice for the lifespan of the era. Today, we know the math is very different. With the expansion of the life expectancy to about 90 years, accumulating a mere 7 to 8 years' worth of salary will likely prove vastly insufficient.

To complicate matters further, saving a significant percentage of one's salary has grown increasingly difficult. Most baby boomers began their careers under the old assumptions, which were based on their parents' models and included pensions, Social Security, and relatively short retirements. Somewhere along the way, however, it became clear that things were changing. Grandparents were living into their eighties! Disciplined savers might have accumulated six or seven years' worth of retirement income, but for the average octogenarian this would not be enough. Mom's and Dad's longer life spans meant more medical and nursing care. As noted in the previous paragraph, our parents and grandparents had, if disciplined, considered six or seven years' worth of income savings to be sufficient for retirement. If Mom or Dad needed nursing care, it was their children who often ended up paying the bill.

Meanwhile, at a campus not far away, in the waning decades of the twentieth century, college tuition escalated at a rate nearly double that of the general economy (rivaled perhaps only by the cost of nursing care). In an increasingly specialized work environment, higher education became an expensive suburban ritual.

The baby boomers are now often referred to as a "sandwich generation" because they are tending financially and emotionally to the needs of those older *and* younger—and at the same time they must figure out how to plan for their own golden years. Future generations are likely to find themselves in a similar crunch.

Increasing longevity presents yet another insidious hurdle that earlier generations didn't have to face. In the previous era (spanning all of the history of humanity), during which retirement was expected to last only a few short years, few retirees had to worry about inflation. Today, however, the prospect of a much longer retirement means that savers must plan for the continual erosion of their buying power. Given the trend toward early retirement, it is no longer unusual for one or both members of a retired couple to be required to live 30 to 40 years off their savings and investments. If we think back over this time frame, a brand new automobile purchased in the early 1970s could have been driven off the lot for about $3,000 and filled with gas at about $.30 a gallon. To adjust for the impact of inflation, today's retirement savers must incorporate some degree of growth into their investing efforts. This consideration unleashes a host of ancillary challenges. The most important is the absolute necessity for taking responsibility for one's retirement planning.

2

Goal Setting

RESPONSIBLE DECISION MAKING begins with having the end in mind.

"I want the highest rate of investment return possible" may be the most dangerous goal an investor can have. This mindset will inevitably lead to potentially catastrophic rearview decision making—something that will be discussed in later chapters. Such investors are doomed to bounce from strategy to strategy seeking an ever elusive outcome.

A far better objective would sound something like this: "I would like the highest rate of return possible given my risk parameters and specifics of my personal goals." Such thinking generally leads to happier places and indeed can serve as a valuable guide along the way. So-called advisors or self-help gurus who do not take these basic considerations into account are probably not worth their cost, even if they are free! Owing to the fact that personal goals are so integral to a responsible planning process, let's spend some time discussing goal setting.

Setting goals for retirement planning purposes begins with four questions.

1. On what date do you wish to retire?
2. How much income will you need during retirement?
3. Do you have financial desires which extend beyond your death, like care for a special-needs dependent, bequest, or another consideration?
4. What is your life expectancy, and (if applicable) that of your spouse?

When deciding when to retire, begin with your ideal target date, then let the ensuing planning provide feedback about whether success is likely. Don't be afraid to revise any of your answers to these questions if this seems called for. It is not uncommon for a well-thought-out game plan to have to adjust to any number of assumed variables. While this is done sometimes because the math indicates that it is required, it should also be done to gain a thorough understanding as to how changes in each of the inputs will affect the outcome.

Many experts suggest that retirees should plan to spend about 75% of their annual working income during their golden years. However, since this factor tends to be the single most important determinant of success, or failure, it is wise to spend some time on this decision. Although most retirees do settle on a figure close to 75% of their working income, my personal experience with clients suggests that the number commonly varies from about *50%* to *over 100%* of working income. How can this be? How can someone spend more money when retired than when working? I call this phenomenon "the Saturday dilemma." When asked to identify the most expensive day of the week, most people will answer Saturday (or Sunday) because on this day they have more time free to spend money. After all, isn't retirement a lot like having 365 Saturdays in a row? So many end up spending more money when they're retired than they did while they were working.

Let's look at a few methods to help get a better idea of what income target might be appropriate for you.

For those who are five years or more away from retiring, the **subtract from gross** method provides valuable feedback. (Anyone who is within five years of retirement might also consider additional methods.) In this calculation we begin by simply adding together the components of *gross* (before tax) income. These might include salary, rent (paid to you), and investment income, such as dividends or interest. However, these items should only be included if you actually spend them as part of your budget. Dividends that are automatically reinvested or rent that is used to pay for expenses of the rental unit itself, for instance, would not be included as part of your gross income for this exercise; these and other such items are instead included in the *asset* (as opposed to *income*) portion of your plan.

From your gross income we then subtract the items that will go away when you retire. This may include the contributions you make to a retirement plan, payments on a mortgage that will be paid off by your target retirement date, FICA (Social Security and Medicare payroll taxes of 7.65% of gross income up to the wage base, as of tax year 2010) or self-employment taxes (double the FICA if you are self-employed), and college savings or expenses (if you are paying for them now and will be done by retirement). A typical scenario might look something like this:

Subtract from Gross Method

Husband's gross pay	$ 50,000	
Wife's gross pay	$ 50,000	
Subtotal		$ 100,000
FICA	–$ 7,650	
Mortgage	–$ 12,000	
401k contribution	–$ 18,000	
Subtotal		–$ 37,650
Gross income target		$ 62,350

Notice that we do not automatically subtract gasoline, car repair, or car payment expenses. This is because many people drive just as much during retirement as they did when they were working—although hopefully the destinations will change.

For those who are within five years of retiring, we suggest that a little more attention be paid to their exact spending habits. A relatively simple means to do this is to establish a single bank account, debit card, or credit card and use this to pay all expenses for one year. It is assumed that credit card balances are paid promptly enough that no finance charges are incurred. Failure to do this may prove unnecessarily costly and indicate potentially significant spending issues. By the end of the designated period, careful planners will have an exact record of their expenses and spending patterns.

Another method involves keeping a notepad with you and writing down everything you spend in a week, or even a month. At the end of the period, not only will you have an excellent idea of what you are spending your money on, but you are likely to become more frugal once you realize that some spur-of-the-moment purchases turn out to be unnecessary.

Don't forget to include seasonal and other non-routine spending that may not show up in your weekly or monthly tabulations, such as annual property taxes, quarterly insurance premiums, holiday expenses, and summer travel.

In calculating how much income you will need in retirement, it is helpful to distinguish between fixed expenses (those which cannot be altered) and discretionary ones. When such fixed expenses as mortgages, other debt payments, utilities, and food represent a significant portion of a couple's retirement spending needs, this must be considered in the income planning process. Income from investments and other sources may sometimes be less than anticipated, so the ability to occasionally cut back on retirement account withdrawals greatly improves the viability of any financial plan. Fixed retirement budget expenses that make up more than 70% of a total spending target may make cutting back a hardship. Those who find themselves with a high fixed-expense ratio may wish to consider making very conservative assumptions as they plan for retirement. They might, for instance, pay special attention to investment vehicles that can provide fixed and dependable income. (This subject is covered in more depth in the *Distribution City* stop on the RetirementQuest.com interactive map and on the RetirementQuest Tool Box link.)

In addition to personal spending targets, some couples have additional monetary goals that fall into the category of **estate planning**. These might include providing for the care of a disabled dependent, leaving a nest egg for future generations, donating to charity, or endowing a special cause. Estate planning is a complex process beyond the scope of this book, but it should be kept in mind while deciding on your income needs and investment strategies for retirement. If you haven't already done so, it is time to consult a qualified attorney who specializes in estate planning.

Our final goal-setting consideration is longevity: how long do you expect your retirement to last? Lifespan has an enormous impact on all aspects of retirement planning. To be safe, planning should provide for enough income to last through the age of 95. Among the challenges that must be considered are the income-robbing effects of inflation, an increased likelihood of spending a significant amount of time in a nursing home or hospital, and the possible changes in Social Security and other entitlement programs. Thorough planning should address these risks, which we will cover in greater detail in the Risk Management chapter of this book.

3

Gather the Information

REATING A FINANCIAL plan begins with compiling your personal inventory of benefits, liabilities, and assets. Every person's inventory is different, but nearly all have some things in common. One is Social Security. For millions of Americans, Social Security remains one of the largest retirement benefits available. According to the U.S. Census Bureau, Social Security benefits are responsible for keeping approximately 33 million seniors out of poverty. Viewed another way, the poverty rate for seniors stood at 8.7% during 2000–2002, but it would have skyrocketed to around 45% without the entitlement program.

When we consider the Social Security Administration's own statistics regarding the tremendous pressures on the program, and indeed a seemingly unavoidable change in the benefit formula, a sobering picture unfolds. The socioeconomic cataclysm that would ensue from the implied dramatic change in the national poverty level leads us to the inevitable conclusion that our own personal vigilance will prove good not only for us, but for the nation as a whole. As a nation we are not yet up to this task. Individuals, government officials, and the financial services industry must commit themselves to taking greater responsibility for our economic well-being as a nation.

To assess your own retirement preparedness, begin by locating your most recent benefit statements. Your current statement can be obtained by contacting the nearest Social Security office or by visiting the Social Security Administration website: www.ssa.gov/mystatement/. It is a good idea to check your annual benefit statement carefully when it arrives. Pay special attention to the History of Earnings section and be sure that the amounts recorded match your actual earnings from the period. If the numbers given are less than what you earned, your employer may be under reporting your earnings, which could result in lower benefits to you. If the reported figure is higher than what you earned, it is possible that someone has stolen your identity, so that their earnings are being posted to your statement. This could be a very serious situation and warrants a call to the proper authorities.

To determine the impact that early retirement or income changes might have on your benefits, you may need to consult a knowledgeable professional like a CERTIFIED FINANCIAL PLANNER™ practitioner or the Social Security Administration itself.

Also essential for planning purposes is a statement for any defined benefit pension for which you are eligible. If you have not received a statement from your employer and any former employers, contact them to request a copy. You have a right to this information and cannot execute a viable retirement plan without it. **Defined benefit pension** refers to the type of benefit which is paid out as a monthly stipend (similar to Social Security). It does not apply to 401k or other cash balance plans, which we will cover later. If you are not sure what type of plan your employer offers, this is a good time to find out. For more information about defined benefit pensions, consult the *Distribution City* section of the RetirementQuest website interactive planning map.

Savings and investment account statements are also important. Simply knowing the approximate balance is not enough, particularly for investment accounts. Careful planning will require such details as fund names, number of shares, and the cost basis of the shares (how much you paid for them). If any of these terms are unfamiliar to you, it might be wise to seek the help of a financial professional or tax advisor.

Debts owed and the details regarding repayment are critical to rendering an accurate assessment of your financial future. Collect summary statements for your mortgage, credit cards, home equity loans, auto loans or leases, and any other liabilities. If you cannot locate a report, call the lender and find out the following details: outstanding balance, interest rate or calculation method, payments, and expected payoff date. If you are missing a single figure for a particular debt, don't worry too much: a skilled consultant should be able to figure out the missing link. For instance, if you know your mortgage balance, interest rate, and monthly payment, it shouldn't be difficult for an advisor to calculate the payoff date.

Although the topic of this book is retirement planning, this is still a good time to locate and review your estate planning documents, including wills, power of attorney, beneficiary designations, trusts, medical directives, and other pertinent information. Entire books have been devoted to estate planning, so here we will only cover the basics. Effective retirement planning should, and in many cases does, result in a **remainder estate** (inheritance for the kids). Estate planning concepts are also covered in the *Final Destination* section of the RetirementQuest website.

4

Crunch the Numbers

ONCE ALL ESSENTIAL information has been gathered and well-thought-out goals have been set, the fun can begin! Most financial advisors use custom software or Web-based programs to "crunch the numbers": to create a financial plan which will provide essential feedback regarding *your* state of financial preparedness. Since this is an integral part of the overall process, here we will spend some time exploring these state-of-the-art planning methods. We will not however, attempt to make you an expert in the minutiae of the planning world. If you intend to do your own planning, you need to fully understand the following broad concepts. Many investors make the dangerous mistake of attempting to master advanced tactics without first understanding the fundamentals. Even if you plan to hire an advisor, it would be prudent to become acquainted with the procedural steps so that you may properly assess the competence and suitability of your prospective advisor. The RetirementQuest.com interactive planning map can help users understand the planning process and thus evaluate their planning efforts.

Remember, the end product can only be as good as the information you put in, so take whatever time is necessary to ensure that your information is as accurate and complete as it can be. When we "crunch the numbers," we apply various assumptions to your hard data. These assumptions involve factors that no one can predict with certainty: your longevity, rates of investment return, taxes, and inflation. Responsible planning dictates that you test your data with more than one set of assumptions. **A forecast that uses only a single set of assumptions may present a dangerously narrow view of your retirement prospects and should not be considered adequate.** Let's consider some scenarios in which failing to consider a wide range of possible futures may prove financially reckless and personally devastating.

Longevity

In this hypothetical example, assume that both members of a newly retired couple are 62 years old. They expect to live to the age of 90. Based on current statistics this seems a reasonable assumption. Let us further assume that *his* Social Security benefit is $25,000 a year, while *hers* is $10,000. In addition, he has a pension based solely on his life which totals $35,000 per year. They also have $300,000 in a 401k plan, from which they intend to withdraw $12,000 annually. If for the purpose of this example we suspend our inflation assumption (see "Inflation," below), we can conclude that this couple could spend $82,000 a year and end up with about twice their initial 401k value, assuming a 6% rate of investment return (see "Investment Rate of Return," on next page).

However, should we change the assumptions and have him unexpectedly die at the age of 64, the widow would run out of money before her 71st birthday!

Inflation

Now let's assume that a 60-year-old couple has diligently amassed a one-million-dollar retirement portfolio. Expecting a 6% rate of return, they plan to withdraw an annual income of $50,000 from their nest egg. Furthermore, they must increase their withdrawal each year to prevent inflation from eroding their buying power and thus their lifestyle. At first glance it might appear sufficient to assume that future inflation will be similar to that of the previous decade: something like 3%. In truth, we don't really know what will happen in the next two or three decades. If our couple withdraws their target amount and increases it by 3% annually, their account will still be worth approximately $384,000 when they reach 90. Now imagine that inflation jumps to an average rate of 6% per year, forcing our couple to withdraw larger sums to maintain their desired lifestyle. In that scenario, they will run out of money when they are only 83!

Investment Rate of Return

Though it might seem likely that a $100,000 investment account earning an average of $8,000 (8%) per year could easily handle annual withdrawals of $5,000 (5%), the wise will remain leery. A straight 8%, earned each and every year without fail, would not only sustain the desired draw rate, but would result in a $143,000 account balance at the end of ten years. Unfortunately, in most time periods and for most investment types, annual returns vary from year to year. Now let's assume a more typical series of returns in which an account records the following returns over a ten-year period:

Year	1	2	3	4	5	6	7	8	9	10
Return %	12	22	17	16	8	-2	6	-6	-10	-15

This hypothetical string of returns also equals an 8% average rate, but at the end of 10 years the ending balance (again assuming annual withdrawals of $5,000) amounts to only $104,000. That's a significant enough difference, but now let's see what happens when we take the exact same year-by-year returns and simply reverse the order in which they occur. The annual withdraw remains the same: $5,000.

Year	1	2	3	4	5	6	7	8	9	10
Return%	-15	-10	-6	6	-2	8	16	17	22	12

In this frightening scenario, the average rate of return is still 8%, but the ending account balance comes in at less than $68,000! In later chapters, when we discuss common investor behavior (or misbehavior), it will become quite clear that making oversimplified assumptions regarding your investment rate of return can lead to a personal planning catastrophe.

These drastically different outcomes based on the same average rate of return illustrate why prudent planners assume a variety of possible scenarios. This way they can anticipate and plan for an array of different outcomes, rather than stake everything on a single "guesstimate." What may not be quite so obvious is that retirees must continually review their progress over the years in the light of their goals and resources. A financial plan should never be viewed as anything other than a snapshot taken at one moment in time. It is more an educational tool than an authoritative mandate.

Financial planning professionals or those non-professionals who choose to take charge of their own planning and investing have state-of-the-art software and other tools at their disposal to help gauge the likelihood of a planning outcome. What this means is that a competent advisor can present several possible outcomes for any plan. A true professional will seek to illustrate both the possible positive and the negative outcomes, because both provide valuable and essential feedback in developing a wise strategy.

In financial planning, **Monte Carlo** refers to a mathematical analysis which attempts to provide an assessment of the relative likelihood that an investment portfolio will successfully serve investor goals. When used properly, a Monte Carlo takes into account portfolio volatility, outside income sources, withdrawal expectations, and all other planning details. In our earlier example, we saw how three portfolios which all had an identical *average* rate of return resulted in very different outcomes. Monte Carlo can help advisors and their clients understand and assess the impact such volatility might have on their planning efforts. In the illustration below we will apply the Monte Carlo method to the examples discussed above. Such an image might look something like this:

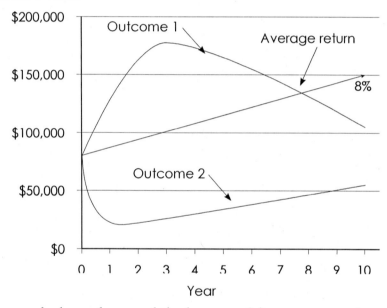

As the graph above shows, while these portfolios experienced nearly identical average returns, once withdrawals were figured in, very different scenarios unfolded.

Monte Carlo simulations can provide even more powerful feedback. Used in its entirety, this analytical method also takes into account the fact that over time a portfolio is very likely to have significantly different rates of return and may produce a result very different from the historical average. Let's consider

some scenarios which include more historically based—
although still hypothetical—returns from the 1990s, and from
the first decade of this new millennium. (For more details on
investment options, including stocks, bonds, mutual funds, and
others, log on to RetirementQuest.com and follow the link to
the RetirementQuest Tool Box.)

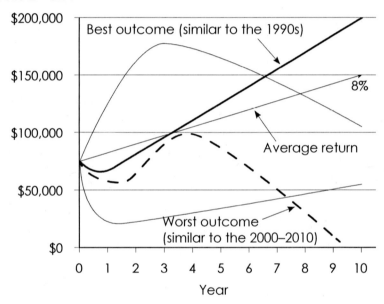

Required Disclosure

Financial Industry Regulatory Authority, Inc. (FINRA®)
requires the following disclosure: "The projections or
other information generated by investment analysis tools
regarding the likelihood of various investment outcomes
are hypothetical in nature, do not reflect actual investment
results and are not guarantees of future results. Results

will vary with each use and over time. Investments not used in a particular simulation may have characteristics similar or even superior to those investments being analyzed. Be sure you are aware of the criteria and methodology used, assumptions made, risk and return parameters used, universe of investments utilized, and limitations. Also, determine how the tool selects securities. And if it favors certain investments, find out how those favorites are determined."

Explanation

FINRA, the industry regulator to which I submitted the manuscript for this book, has a difficult task. To ensure that complicated financial subject matter be presented in the fairest possible way, appropriate disclosures must cover all conceivable situations. This necessitates complicated wording that can overwhelm the financial novice. The following represents my personal read on the spirit and intent of the above disclosure.

- In general, the Monte Carlo method is best used in conjunction with widely accepted risk (standard deviation) and return characteristics of the broad market indexes (e.g., S&P 500 index) for the purpose of overall financial planning and not for specific selection of a stock, mutual fund, or other security. Also, the output from this tool should not be considered a rock solid prediction of any outcome but rather a general educational illustration to help planners understand the broadest possible picture.

- When used properly this simulation will give somewhat different results each time used and so should be run several times to garner the best possible understanding.
- There will always be some individual investments that perform better than average, and they may do so for a long time. On the other hand, there will always be some investments that perform worse than average, and they may do so for a long time. Now here is the gem of wisdom: history tells us very little about what might happen *next*; so it is extremely difficult (even for professionals) to know in advance which will be which. My opinion has always been that if your financial plan requires you to get a higher than average return on your portfolio, then you should seriously reconsider your goals.
- Due to the potentially large number of variables to a financial plan, any tool designed to simulate possible outcomes can result in costly mistakes if misused. Whether by error or something more sinister, illustrations using skewed data or limited investment parameters may not give a realistic depiction. Again, always stick with the broadest measures, and only use widely accepted historical risk and return assumptions.

Sound a bit overwhelming? For most people it may very well be; so don't be afraid to ask your advisor questions;

and if you are still unsure, seek a second opinion (always a good idea anyway).

When we add in the historically based returns of the '90s (heavy solid curve) and the '00s (dashed curve), a very useful picture begins to emerge. We can now see that a portfolio which is *designed* to achieve an 8% rate of return, and from which we intend to withdraw 5% annually, could result in a wide range of possible outcomes, anywhere from stellar growth to virtual collapse. A true Monte Carlo would add thousands of return scenarios, each ideally based upon an accurate, in-depth assessment of your portfolio and your retirement expectations, and would culminate in a percentage. For example, based upon the information in the previous graph, we might get a 75% Monte Carlo output. What this means is that of the thousands of instantaneous samples run, 75% *did not* result in an unacceptable outcome at the end of the time period.

A flag of caution should be raised whenever your planning produces a Monte Carlo result below 70%. This might be a passing grade in grade-school math, but almost all financial planners consider any result below this level to be a failure—or, more simply stated, too risky. If you conduct your own assessment, pay special attention to the measure of risk utilized (standard deviation), because small changes to this variable are very likely to result in significant differences in the final results. If you are not already familiar with this term, it's time to do some research—or to consult a competent financial planner who understands the challenges of risk management.

As we study the graphs on the next three pages, important details emerge. Perhaps most significant is the fact that although

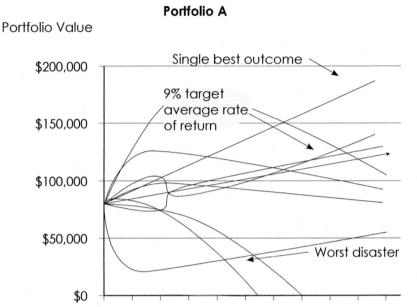

Portfolio A

Portfolio Value

Single best outcome

$200,000

9% target average rate of return

$150,000

$100,000

$50,000

Worst disaster

$0

0 1 2 3 4 5 6 7 8 9 10

Year

an aggressive portfolio (A) which is designed to target high rates of return does indeed achieve the highest long-term *average* return, and produce the single absolute best possible outcome, it also produces the worst financial disasters. By contrast, in examples A and B, a more modest portfolio (B) *lessened* the best possible outcome, but it also *improved* the worst-case scenarios. Finally we can see that (C), a portfolio which successfully targeted very low volatility risk, failed in almost all cases to produce enough growth to enable long-term success. While these scenarios are purely hypothetical, they do represent common planning results. It is important to remember that your own circumstances may vary greatly from these examples.

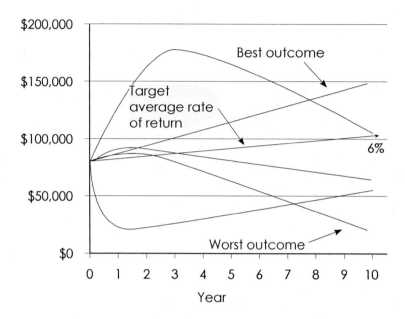

Portfolio B

Portfolio Value

Best outcome

Target average rate of return

6%

Worst outcome

Year

In the real world, Monte Carlo simulations are often used, I believe inappropriately, to *sell* investment products or programs. Unfortunately there exist far too many variables and limitations for this tool to be considered a sole basis on which to reliably make investment decisions. It should be considered, however, to be a valuable resource to gauge the overall feasibility of your financial planning efforts. Also, if you re-run your simulation and find a slightly different outcome, don't be alarmed, as the built-in random number generation feature should be expected to bring about such a result. Remember, this tool is designed for *big picture* feedback, not so much for micro-details. Finally, investors should be aware that certain individual investments, as opposed to the broadly diversified

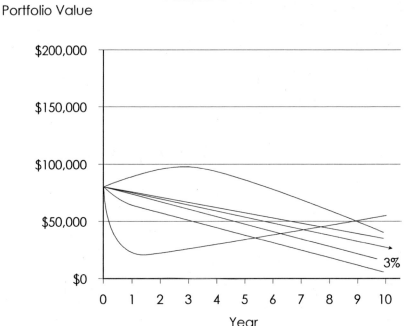

Portfolio C

Portfolio Value

examples that are regularly discussed in this book, may have better outcomes. It is also true however, that those same individual investments may have *far* worse results, including total loss, which is why this book only addresses diversified portfolios.

Another common method to test the validity, or associated risk, of your retirement plan involves **back-testing.** Back-testing means asking how your portfolio would have fared in the same investment markets in an earlier decade. For example, an investor who expects to retire with a given withdrawal scenario and with a portfolio consisting half of stocks and half of bonds might look at how this investment strategy would have worked in particular historical periods.

Periods that were especially challenging for investors, like the pre-World War II years, the early 1970s, and the dot-com bust period, would be used to gauge how well the strategy might hold up during a similar future market event. It is especially imperative to measure the impact of a challenging market on the *early* phases of a retirement scenario because, as discussed earlier, events in this period often have significant impact on later outcomes.

5

Adjustments

S O WHAT COMES next? That depends largely on the feedback coming in from your planning efforts. Although I typically only counsel those who have decided to visit a professional advisor, I find that a surprisingly large percentage of those who execute a plan end up with a favorable result. This means that the combination of goals, assumptions, and resources result in a workable scenario, one with a comfortably high likelihood of attaining the stated objectives. It does not mean that nothing else need be done. Let's take a moment to review a few common situations.

The first situation we will consider is overabundance. Make no mistake: this is a good problem to have. For example, assume that a couple is preparing to retire at age 65 and has a $2 million nest egg. After carefully crunching the numbers, they and their financial advisor determine that it is likely that not only will they have enough income to last their entire lives but they will leave a significant estate to their children. In fact, their austere spending habits result in a portfolio which will likely grow throughout their golden years, even assuming a very conservative rate of investment return. Thus the couple may want to consider adjusting their goals or the strategies they have adopted to achieve them. Some possibilities: adjust their investment strategy to seek less volatile (although slower) rates of growth, retire earlier, or spend more money once they are retired. To their original goals they might add making gifts to children or grandchildren, reducing future estate tax, and lifetime tax efficiency—a strategy which considers tax ramifications throughout one's life and not just for the next installment of April 15th (see the *Tax Law Quagmire* section on the RetirementQuest.com interactive planning map).

But what about you? What if your current conglomeration of goals, resources and assumptions *do not* result in a favorable outcome? In this situation, you have four principal options. A change in goals is perhaps the most obvious. Revisit your ideal retirement date; perhaps working a few extra years will improve your prospects. Look at the income target you have set. While it is not realistic to just resolve to spend less money in retirement, most people find that upon close inspection there is often some leeway in this area. If you choose this path, be sure to practice living on the target income *before* you retire. This is a good idea in almost every planning situation.

The third option is to change your planning *assumptions* about rate of return, inflation, taxes, and the like. If you contemplate doing this, you should exercise great caution and research your decisions thoroughly. A frequent target for alteration is the portfolio's rate of return. While there is evidence to suggest that increasing the equity (stock) holdings in a portfolio has historically resulted in higher growth over time (stocks and bonds will be covered in a later chapter), it is also true that such a strategy will significantly increase the short-term volatility (a type of risk), thereby increasing the day-to-day gyrations in the account value. Think through your options carefully, and refer back to the earlier discussions of the Monte Carlo simulations.

The final possibility that might help improve a less-than-ideal forecast is to change the resources available. For younger workers, this might be as simple as choosing the job with a matching 401k over similar employment which offers no such benefit. The most common strategy for improving available resources is to increase one's contribution to 401k or other company retirement plan investments, or to start contributing if one isn't already doing so. Those within a few years of retiring will probably find it difficult to make a great impact by saving more, but younger people can significantly improve their lot by taking a disciplined approach to savings.

I cannot overstate the importance of the 401k in retirement wealth building. At this writing, I have been advising clients for nearly twenty years, and in that time the value of a payroll-deducted approach has been obvious. In those two decades I have advised people from all walks of life and with all manner of goals and aspirations. For many, I have become intricately involved in their lives and have monitored their progress through some very good investment periods and some very frightening ones. What I have observed is that most people, no matter how scared or financially strapped, will not alter their 401k (or 403b) investment program—except to increase the amount they are saving. As a result, most of the individuals and couples whom I advise and who also utilize an employer-based plan are essentially on track to pursue their goals. On the other hand, I have noticed that those who fail to commit to a payroll-deducted strategy, or who do not have access to one, have generally experienced far poorer results. Lacking the automatic discipline inherent to a program in which your employer automatically withholds your contribution from your paycheck, most savers will simply spend the money or fall prey to one of the common investor mistakes which we will discuss in other chapters.

How important could that really be? In the late summer of 2009, a time at which the stock market remained about 20% below its peak of two years earlier, a prominent mutual fund company announced that its 401k customers actually posted gains for the period. To better understand this phenomenon, known as **dollar-cost averaging**, consider the example on the next page.

Notice that during the periods when share prices were down, the investor was able to accumulate *more* shares at the lower price and, conversely, *fewer* shares at the higher prices. While some results would likely differ, in this example the resulting profit on the low-priced shares was sufficient to compensate for the losses on the higher-priced ones. When we compare this hypothetical scenario with the Monte Carlo examples, the results seem contradictory. In the Monte Carlo example, volatility appeared to harm the investment outcome, while in this scenario it has boosted the portfolio's rate of return. The key difference between the examples lies in which direction the money is moving. In the Monte Carlo scenarios, investors were taking money *out* of their portfolios, while with dollar-cost averaging money was flowing *into* the portfolio. I **think the conclusion to be drawn is that the day-to-day (or year-**

An investor puts one hundred dollars a month into his 401k over the course of one year. During this period (shaded rows), the stock market loses half of its value due to a severe economic blow and then proceeds to regain some of the losses. By year's end, the market is worth about 20% less than it was at the beginning. The hypothetical investor, however, has made a profit. Here's how:

Amount invested	share price	# shares purchased
$100	$50	2
$100	$50	2
$100	$33	3
$100	$33	3
$100	$25	4
$100	$25	4
$100	$20	5
$100	$20	5
$100	$25	4
$100	$25	4
$100	$33	3
$100	$40	2.5
Total: $1,200 (cost)		41.5

and

$ 40 (ending stock price)
× 41.5 (number of shares owned)
= $1,660 (portfolio value)

Note: Dollar cost averaging does not protect against a loss or ensure a profit.

to-year) fluctuations in the investment markets may provide valuable long-term growth opportunities for disciplined investors who are putting money into their portfolios, but those same gyrations can become quite problematic for those retirees who are withdrawing income from their accounts.

IMPORTANT

Please be aware, as noted in the chart on the facing page, that dollar cost averaging does not protect against a loss in declining markets. In fact, for most of the years illustrated, the hypothetical investment would have represented a loss if cashed in. Therefore, an investor should very carefully consider their time horizon in conjunction with a dollar cost averaging approach.

Unfortunately, some individuals and couples have to confront a third planning outcome. Rather than overabundance or a plan which merely requires some tweaking, they do not have nearly enough resources to generate a workable retirement outcome. The challenges facing these people are beyond the scope of this book. This book is intended for mature readers who have already achieved a reasonable level of financial security and responsibility, and for younger people who are actively in a wealth building mode.

Any financial plan presentation or investment strategy which indicates a workable outcome should immediately be followed by the following question: what could go wrong? Risk management then becomes the next logical step in the lifelong commitment to financial responsibility.

6

Risk Management

F OR THOSE IN the business world, the term *risk management* conjures images of a diverse set of activities and solutions. However, for the average homeowner what comes to mind is usually someone trying to sell them insurance. Insurance is indeed an integral part of risk management, but it is only one piece of a broad and intricate puzzle. The insurance industry sells risk abatement. It is important to realize that not all risks can be insured against, and that buying an insurance policy is not always the most efficient solution even for those cases in which insurance is generally appropriate. In addition, insurance salesmen posing as objective advisors have sometimes been known to suggest expensive policies when they are not called for. Here we will focus on the *appropriate* uses of insurance, as well as non-insurance strategies to typical risk patterns.

While few question the benefit of life insurance in protecting the family in the event of a tragic loss of a breadwinner, seldom does the topic of disability protection arise. In fact, according to 2009 data from the Life and Health

Insurance Foundation for Education, at some point during their career nearly one in five Americans will suffer a disability lasting up to one year. Disability policies cover an individual for lost wages, provided certain conditions are met. To start with, I suggest taking the following steps:

- Determine what, if any, disability insurance is provided by your employer.
- Consult a financial advisor to determine what impact lost wages would have on your life, or run your own analysis if you feel competent to do so.
- If a disability would adversely affect your finances, consult a disability insurance expert to determine what policy is best for you.

Insurance policies differ widely in coverage, benefits, and cost. Don't be afraid to shop around. Get more than one quote, and let the agents know you are doing so. This will help ensure that each gives you a competitive price; you will probably find also that the sales representatives are more than willing to point out any shortcomings in what their competitors are offering.

Disability coverage, of course, is not the only important form of protection to consider. To protect a family against the catastrophic loss of a breadwinner, few tools fit the bill like life insurance. However, life insurance policies come in different types, including term, whole life, and universal life. Which type is appropriate for you? Let's review the differences.

Term life insurance is pure death benefit protection. As the name implies, these policies are valid for a specified time period, after which renewal is required. There are many variations, most of which are described in the contract name. For example, **annual renewable term** (ART) refers to a policy in which premiums are renewed each year. As a result, in the early years premiums are quite low compared to most other policy types, but as the insured (you) ages the cost increases. Other policies are described in terms of the number of years for which premiums remain constant. So **ten-year term** would describe a policy with premiums contractually stable for a period of ten years. The vast majority of term policies never pay a death benefit, for the simple reason that they are designed to become prohibitively expensive for aging policyholders. To be fair, they are not *designed* to do this; rather, this is a consequence of their purpose. Term policies are the type of life coverage that comes closest to pure insurance. Remember that insurance is an arrangement whereby the policy issuer (the insurance company) absorbs risk on behalf of the premium payer (you). With term life, the insurer is mitigating the financial risk of the loss of a breadwinner. As the policy owner ages, the risk of death increases and therefore the premium cost does too. This seems fair to me.

So why would someone buy a policy which will probably become prohibitively expensive long before it is time to collect? And why did your insurance agent never mention term policies? The answer to both questions is the same: term insurance is dirt cheap, especially for the young and healthy. In fact, it is so inexpensive that most insurance agents cannot make a living selling term policies. However, this book was not written for insurance agents, unless they are planning for their retirement. For consumers, the benefit is that many people can afford *appropriate* levels of term coverage. After all, the risk of losing a breadwinner is most dramatic financially when a family is young. As we age, and hopefully accumulate assets and resources, the need for high death benefits may very well decrease. When investors reach a certain net worth, especially in 401k and other cash assets, many come to feel they are *self-insured*. However, great care should be taken before canceling any insurance policy. Always ask yourself the following question: What would happen if I canceled and then died or got sick and uninsurable? A good financial advisor or do-it-yourself software can model the scenario in order to help answer that critical question.

So, just how cheap is term insurance? The monthly premium cost for term insurance can be as much as 90% less than comparable whole life policies and 20% of the cost of some universal life policies. In other words, a policy owner who could only afford $100,000 in whole life coverage could instead purchase almost a million dollars' worth of term insurance. Believe me, if you have ever counseled a young widow who is attempting to pick up the pieces and live off of insurance proceeds, then you know that a million-dollar benefit is *a lot* better than a hundred-thousand-dollar benefit!

So then why would anybody purchase a whole life policy, and why are they so expensive? Whole life policies, as the name implies, are designed to provide coverage throughout the duration of a person's life, and ultimately they pay a death benefit. Therefore, people who desire a death benefit when they die at a ripe old age may find it appropriate to pay higher premiums for the additional risk mitigation. What additional risk mitigation, you might ask? The average whole life policy guarantees a death benefit regardless of market factors, as long as premiums are paid. In other words, it does not matter what the stock market does, how interest rates move, or at what age you die: the company will provide a death benefit without raising premiums. (Keep in mind, however, that policies vary and therefore the details need be confirmed.) Also, almost all insurers retain the right to raise premiums (your cost) if necessary, but this can generally only be done for an entire class of policies, not on an individual basis. Since longevity has increased steadily over the last several decades, most insurers have not raised policy rates. In fact, many have lowered their premiums.

What about whole life insurance as an investment? Is it ever appropriate? Generally I answer this question with "no." However, under some circumstances I may offer different advice. For those who desire a cash benefit at the end of their life, are very conservative investors, and can afford the cash premiums—then whole life insurance might make some sense as an investment. In my planning practice, when studying whole life contracts we generally find very similar patterns, which look something like the illustration on the opposite page, which is not indicative of all policies.

Once again, while the details vary from one policy to the next, using this general guideline we can draw some meaningful conclusions. For short- to medium-term investing, life insurance represents a poor choice. For the longer term, whole life contracts can generally prove competitive with other cash-type investments. In addition, while a new investment in life insurance *might* not be wise, those who hold older contracts may not wish to get rid of them. For example, assume that a young man invests $100 a month in a whole life

Phase	Cash Surrender Value	Dividend Accrual	Death Benefit
Early years (years 1–12)	Negative	Negligible	Much higher than cash value
Middle years	Break even	Meaningful	Significantly higher than cash value
Late years (years 20+)	Positive (2–4%)	Attractive	Similar to cash value

insurance policy (which might result in a death benefit value of approximately $100,000), $100 a month in a term life policy (with a death benefit of $1 million), and $100 a month in a 401k account. Should he die early, the whole life insurance death benefit would almost certainly be worth more than the 401k, but also considerably less than the term policy. Should he live for 30 years and retire, the term policy would likely already have been canceled due to prohibitive premium costs, and the whole life contract would provide $100,000 should he die, but a considerably less cash value amount should he be living.

Meanwhile, the 401k value, given the tax advantages and likely superior growth rates, would almost certainly exceed the value of the whole life insurance death benefit *or* its cash value.[2] This does not mean, however, that at this point he should cash in the whole life policy. Dividend growth in a whole life policy, while slow in the early and middle years, increases significantly in the later years, so that it (eventually) becomes quite competitive with cash-type investments. Also, it is likely that this man, no longer young, may desire more conservative investments. Therefore, while a young person might be ill advised to use life insurance simply for an investment, once the policy has been in force for many years, there could be good reason to hold on to it.

Universal life insurance can be thought of as a hybrid of term and whole life insurance contracts. Similar to whole life, universal policies are *designed* to provide a benefit throughout life. Unlike whole life, however, the outcome of the policy is not guaranteed by the issuer; instead, the contract values are dependent upon investment performance and acquired age. In essence, universal life is a savings account from which term insurance costs are drawn. *With favorable investment performance* there will exist sufficient reserves from which to draw the high risk charges associated with older age; otherwise, with unfavorable investment results, the policy lapses and becomes worthless. It is important to remember that universal life policies are based upon assumptions rather than guarantees, and therefore require ongoing monitoring.

While there are important considerations regarding estate and tax planning as they relate to life insurance, we will limit our focus (for now) to the issues discussed above. As pointed out earlier, risk management does go beyond simply buying insurance policies. Risk tolerance can play a vital role in portfolio management and in an investor's overall quality of life. To more fully appreciate this statement, try talking to someone who inappropriately managed portfolio risk by, say, staking everything on the dot-com fiasco of 2000–2002. You will likely find that not just money was lost but, in many cases that I have seen, self-esteem, optimism, and even the health of many marriages.

Most investors have at least some experience with risk-tolerance questionnaires—the five- or six-question version which solicits self-assessing responses. Allow me to offer an observation about these mini-assessments: human behavior is far too complex to be evaluated on the basis of a five-minute questionnaire! An *experienced* financial advisor might allow as much as one full hour to gauge a client's risk tolerance. A *great* advisor will continue to assess your risk tolerance for as long as you have a relationship! In short, I believe the five-minute risk-tolerance questionnaire is primarily designed to protect the investment company from allegations that it has sold products to inappropriate investors.

The primary problem with the instant evaluations is that they tend to measure risk *perception*, rather than risk *tolerance*. Risk *perception* involves how likely you think it is that an unpleasant outcome will occur. Risk *tolerance* is a measure of how comfortable you are with risk, or your ability to tolerate unexpected and unwanted outcomes. While individual risk *tolerance* tends to remain relatively consistent over time, risk *perception* changes with a high degree of regularity. Millions of American investors, failing to comprehend the distinction, reported a high tolerance for risk during the technology-stock boom of the late 1990s. This report was due largely to the nonstop media coverage which led many investors to believe that the stock market was sure to continue to ratchet skyward. As a result, the general *perception* of risk was greatly affected, but that did not necessarily translate to a cultural increase in risk *tolerance*. This fact was borne out when in February of 2000 the market began a multiyear decline, causing investors to head for the exits in record numbers, but only after they had already lost significant wealth. Those who had truly high risk-tolerance levels, however, aggressively *bought* stocks throughout the tumble; in the belief that shares were priced at rock-bottom levels. Unfortunately, according to the common mini-assessment, these two types of investors were treated exactly the same by any brokers or no-load mutual fund companies who might have served them, yet their experiences and outcomes differed drastically! It is likely that some investors, rather than having a high risk *tolerance*, instead had a *perception* that there was little or no risk. These investors panicked when the market went into freefall. Conversely, those investors who had a genuinely high tolerance for risk were generally not put off by the bursting of the tech bubble, and most were attracted by the opportunity to buy low-priced shares.

If you plan to work with an advisor, pay particular attention to the risk-tolerance arena. A good advisor should not only go beyond the simple questionnaire, but continually ask and even challenge you about your relationship with investment risk. If you plan to tackle the job yourself, be sure to maintain a constant vigilance and reconsider these issues regularly. In general, I have found that people with high *investment* risk tolerance levels tend to have a high tolerance for risk in other aspects of their lives, and vice versa. This notion bears repeating: Mistakes in risk-tolerance assessment often lead to mistakes in investor behavior, which can lead in turn to catastrophic investment errors.

Perhaps the most useful application of risk tolerance involves an investor's asset allocation model. **Asset allocation** is the art of diversifying your portfolio to include various investments carefully chosen in an effort to produce a balancing effect. The goal of asset allocation is to create a portfolio which generates sufficient growth to meet an investor's long-term goals, while reducing short-term volatility (a type of risk) to acceptable levels. The government provides a beginner's guide to asset allocation at www.sec.gov/investor/pubs/assetallocation .htm.

The Efficient Frontier, based upon the Nobel Prize–winning work of Harry Markowitz, illustrated the beneficial effects of proper asset mixes. The study demonstrated that the risk-return relationship is a nonlinear equation. As investors add portfolio holdings with higher growth potential, they also inadvertently increase the short-term volatility of their investment. At certain high levels, additional increases in risk no longer add to long-term returns, but will detract from them. Graphically the scenario is depicted something like this hypothetical example:

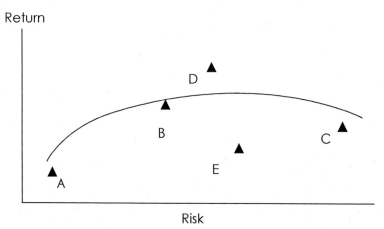

Required Disclosure Illustration only. Not indicative of any investment or investing result. Asset allocation does not guarantee against investor loss, and non-diversified portfolios may produce better results.

As you can see, starting at point A, as we add risk to the mix, we are proportionately rewarded with higher potential returns. However, once we reach a certain risk level (B), the additional return starts to diminish. Eventually, when we add excessive risk (C), we actually begin to reduce the expected long-term returns of the portfolio. In addition, it is not likely for a portfolio to exist above the "efficient frontier" (D) for any length of time, since by definition the frontier represents the highest possible return for a given risk level. The common term for scenario (D) is "bubble," suggesting that an implosion of some form is due. Portfolios below the frontier (E) can be said to be either taking too much risk for a given level of return or achieving low returns for a given level of risk. Portfolio (B), in this example, could be described as an optimal portfolio, although only appropriate for investors who are seeking high long-term growth and who are willing to experience significant short-term volatility (a form of risk). Meanwhile; concentrated portfolios, or those composed of a large proportion of a limited number of holdings, may produce higher returns during a given time period (as with D), but also possess a greater possibility for extreme or even total loss as compared to a diversified and asset allocated approach.

Our goal is to now have arrived at a retirement planning scenario that is believed likely to come to fruition. The next step in the process is portfolio management. Unlike the earlier steps, which are labor-intensive at the beginning but generally become less so over time, portfolio management demands ever more attention as time goes on, and is indeed critical for those nearing retirement.

7

Risk in a Modern World

F OR THE PURPOSE of this and all future discussions, we
will assume that investors fully understand the necessity
for diversification in their investing efforts. As the
employees of Enron, loyal to the end, discovered, a non-
diversified investment runs the unique risk of total loss. They
held company stock in their individual 401k portfolios; in fact,
approximately 62% of the assets in the Enron plan were Enron
stock. A sudden and tragic loss of this magnitude cannot be
made up over time (except possibly by the very young) and will
almost certainly end in hardship for those caught in the tumult.

Yet the phenomenon of overconcentration, or lack
of diversification, surfaces time and again in the investing
vernacular. The 401k may be the single most common example
of this investing pitfall. Reasons for overexposure to company
stock may include employer contribution matches, automatic
default investment choices, or simple lack of awareness.
The most common reason, however, is familiarity. When
interviewed, those whose portfolios were overconcentrated in
their own employer's stock often cited comfort as the reason.

They have come to believe in that company, which, after all, has over the years reliably issued paychecks, thrown holiday parties, and provided other benefits. Most Enron employees indicated that they thought their company and management were superior to those of industry peers. As in other cases, these frontline workers were the last to know that they had been taken in by an alleged managerial snow job.

Company retirement plans that rely too heavily on the company's own stock are by no means the only common source of dangerous portfolio overconcentration. Another one is what I call the "winner syndrome." For example, investors may purchase, inherit, or otherwise come into possession of a basket of stocks that have a limited degree of diversification. However, over time, one or two holdings may outperform the others, and when compounded for 20 or so years they may grow to dominate the overall portfolio. The problem is that due to the length of time generally required, the dangers associated with portfolio overconcentration may materialize just at the point at which the investor comes to rely on the portfolio for retirement purposes.

Human emotion often leads us to become attached to the winner. We may have a good feeling every month when we look at our investment account statements or cash a dividend check. In my own planning practice I have listened to clients describe their favorite portfolio holdings as their best friend, their mistress, or even their children. One investor even confessed to having a better relationship with his favorite stocks than with his own offspring. Besides—the company's management must know something in order to get such superior performance, right? Many company stocks do indeed outperform others based on the grand vision and acumen of their managers, but there are other, less laudable reasons that one stock might outperform another, such as the excessive corporate risk-taking that characterized the various recent debacles associated with the banking sector.

Other contributors to *seemingly* superior stock price performance include the kind of investor mania we experienced during the dot-com era (we will cover this in more depth in another chapter), or outright corporate fraud.

So how does one avoid a dangerous overconcentration? There are a number of ways to counteract the risks associated with this peril, but the simplest, and by far the most common, is to develop and maintain a diversified portfolio, or, as grandmother counseled, to not put all your eggs into one basket. Likely the most familiar to savers is the mutual fund, which is a large pool of investor money used to purchase a number of different stocks, bonds, or other assets. Even a portfolio that comprises a single mutual fund is generally numerically diversified; this helps reduce the risk associated with overconcentration in a single stock. The typical mutual fund might have a couple of dozen different holdings or as many as a couple of hundred. (Mutual funds are offered by prospectus, which should be read for expense and other important details prior to investing.) By choosing a number of funds with different objectives and underlying holdings, an investor can almost eliminate the type of cataclysmic risk associated with overconcentration. **While this in no way guarantees that all forms of risk will be avoided, we will assume going forward that responsible savers achieve at least this entry level of risk mitigation for their serious money.**

Professional financial advisors are often asked "Is there any risk?" Responsible investing requires that we acknowledge that there is *always* risk. For example, many savers assume that a bank certificate of deposit (CD) or other cash investment has no risk at all. While it is accurate to say that these instruments have no *market* risk, meaning that there is no possibility of a short-term loss due to market fluctuations, they might very well pose a risk to an individual's planning efforts. If such an investment is intended solely to generate retirement income and it only yields a paltry 2–3% in interest payments, the investor would likely find himself or herself forced to invade principal in order to make ends meet—assuming that the person has an average lifespan. Once the savings were exhausted, the very real risk of going broke would be realized. Other investment alternatives, such as a diversified portfolio yielding 5%, although subject to short-term fluctuations, might have produced enough interest payments to cover living expenses and thereby overcome the risk of running out of money. See the illustration on the opposite page.

As we can see, while Choice 1, the CD, has no principal or interest-rate risk, it did not bring about the desired planning outcome: 35 years of income and a meaningful inheritance for the kids. In contrast, in Choice 2, the value of the investment did suffer meaningful short-term setbacks (note years 1 through 10 and again 20 through 30), but the couple did meet both of their desired goals: drawing an annual income and leaving their children a meaningful nest egg. Note that this is an oversimplified example because it does not take into account taxes, inflation, and other considerations that are crucial to responsible planning.

Let's assume that a retired couple has $500,000 to invest and needs to draw an income from this investment of at least $25,000 a year to fund retirement needs. Further, assume that they expect to live for 35 years in retirement and would like to leave as much as possible to their children as an inheritance.

Choice 1: Invest in a bank CD earning 2.2% interest.

Choice 2: Invest in a diversified portfolio of bonds yielding 5%.

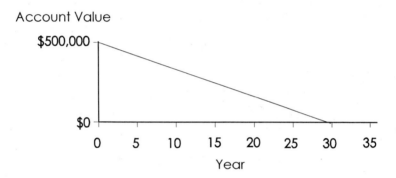

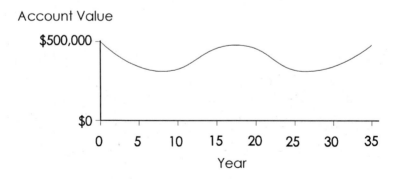

These illustrations are oversimplified to show volatility. They are not indications of any actual investment and not guarantees of any investing result

Required Disclosure

The purchase of bonds is subject to availability and market conditions. Generally, the bond market is volatile; bond prices rise when interest rates fall and vice versa. Market risk is a consideration if bonds are sold or redeemed prior to maturity. Some bonds have call features that may affect income. Corporate bonds contain elements of both interest-rate risk and credit risk. Government bonds are guaranteed only as to timely payment of principal and interest and do not eliminate market risk.

Explanation

The regulations require all of this verbiage to immediately follow any discussion of bonds. I choose to take several pages to explain these concepts and do so in chapter 9. Please stay tuned.

Responsible risk-management planning must go further than "Is it risky?" With the average person now shouldering so much of the burden for his or her own retirement years, it becomes imperative that we learn to ask such questions as "What risks are entailed and what risks are alleviated by a given approach?" Before these questions can be addressed, investors need to understand the characteristics of basic investments.

8

Investing

WHILE THERE ARE many aspects of portfolio management, we will assume that investors strive for a well-thought-out portfolio mix that enables them to meet their long-term goals and sufficiently matches their true risk tolerance. Once this has been achieved, the most important, ongoing risk-management tool becomes investment-account rebalancing. *Rebalancing* means monitoring your investment mix and making adjustments as necessary to remain on course toward your target. Due to the ceaseless gyrations known as the market cycle (which we will cover in greater depth in later chapters), certain investments might behave very well for a considerable period of time, perhaps a decade or more. During these periods, such assets might appear to reside above the efficient frontier, as did the dot-com stocks, real estate, bank shares, and oil contracts in their respective cycles. You should be aware that I find **it is precisely at these moments that the media will pound investors with the news that "it really is different this time."** Brokers and other sales folks are also likely to point to "hot performance" as a reason to load up on more shares.

Account rebalancing is a much better strategy for weathering these storms. If your plan and your portfolio are sound, your challenge is to muster the courage required to ignore the din and simply rebalance your portfolio. Allow me to illustrate with an example.

Assume that after careful planning an investor determines that her ideal mix of assets is half in stocks and the other half in bonds. Further, imagine that this investor does not currently need to withdraw any money from her portfolio. The market enters a tumultuous time period during which stocks do very well, then perform horrifically, and then recover some of their declines—not unlike the markets of 1997–2003. Also during this time period, bonds often went up when stocks declined and declined when stocks went up. Let's further assume that our hypothetical investor rebalanced her portfolio at the end of each year, and that shares of both the chosen stock *and* bond funds were initially trading at $10 apiece. A $1 million starting account balance might have behaved something like this:

						Result		
Year	$ Stock	%	$ Bond	%	Rebalance action	$ Stock	$ Bond	$ Total
Start	500,000		500,000					
1997	665,000	33	550,000	10	sell $57,500 stock	607,500	607,500	1,215,000
1998	857,850	41	662,175	9	sell $97,838 stock	760,012	760,012	1,520,024

						Result		
Year	$ Stock	%	$ Bond	%	Rebalance action	$ Stock	$ Bond	$ Total
1999	919,614	21	752,411	−1	sell $83,601 stock	836,012	836,012	1,672,024
2000	827,651	−9	936,333	12	buy $54,341 stock	881,992	881,992	1,763,984
2001	776,153	−12	952,551	8	buy $88,199 stock	864,352	864,352	1,728,704
2002	674,194	−22	950,787	10	buy $138,296 stock	812,491	812,491	1,624,982
2003	1,048,112	29	928,190	4	sell $59,961 stock	988,151	988,151	1,976,302

Over the seven-year period, the average compounded
rate of return experienced by the hypothetical stock fund
came in at 9%, while the bond fund returned 7.35%. The
rebalanced portfolio, however, experienced meaningfully
higher performance at 10.22%. Although these are made-up
investments, they closely approximate the characteristics of the
time period. When disciplined rebalancing was applied, the
overall portfolio actually achieved higher returns than either of
its component parts. This is a very powerful message; there are
additional interpretations which can prove equally valuable.

During this period the bond account only had a
single year of negative returns, yet it also significantly
underperformed both the stock account *and* the combined
portfolio for the total period. The conclusion could be drawn
that for investors who do not need more than a 5–7% rate of
return and possess a low risk tolerance, the reduced volatility
associated with bonds might indicate a bond-heavy portfolio

prescription. Not so obvious is the observation that during the single negative return period for bonds (1999), a portfolio which included a small percentage of stocks (perhaps as low as 10%) would have eliminated all portfolio losses and improved growth rates for the duration of the example. **In most cases adding a small percentage of a different investment type will help reduce volatility and may very well improve long-term performance. (This is also a tenet of the efficient frontier and modern portfolio theory.)** However, for those individuals who after careful planning determine that they may require a higher return than can be achieved with bonds, it could also be said that the evenly blended portfolio greatly reduced the volatility associated with stocks while providing a more appropriate higher return. Finally, if we look at the results column, it becomes clear that although the combined portfolio experienced more loss years than the bonds, those declines were significantly muted as compared with the pure stock investment.

However, this is not the whole story. Perhaps the most significant path on this particular journey involves the real-world application of rebalancing theory. In order to fully comprehend this, it is helpful to consider investor behavior. Investors are often tempted to make the worst possible move, at the worst possible moment. Notice that it could be claimed that during the years 1997–1999 stocks were the best investment. The three-year compounded return for our example averaged 31.4% compared to the paltry 5.9% posted by the bonds. During such a period talking heads on television would have spouted this observation nonstop. Worse yet, financial salespeople of all ilks unfurled charts and graphs suggesting that you must not *miss the boat*. After all, they pitched, this may be a once in a lifetime opportunity and, most important, *things are different this time.* (Historically speaking this statement has almost always been followed by classically bad investment advice.[3]) The pearl embedded in the clammy sales pitch, they implied, was the promise of higher rates of investment return. We were bombarded with enthusiastic pronouncements: It's a new economy! We are in uncharted waters! Modern technology will enable limitless stock market growth!

So investors in record-setting numbers dumped their bond holdings (in 1999) and blindly poured their money into stocks.[4] Referring back to the example above, you will notice that 1999 turned out to be a less-than-ideal moment to dump bonds and buy stocks. The rest of the story, so often overlooked until it is too late, is that **any attempt to get higher rates of return than a well-constructed portfolio must, by definition, also increase risk.** Unfortunately for them, investors who held bonds between 1997 and 1999 and then exchanged them for stocks did not experience a seven-year return of 10.22%, 9.00%, or even 7.35%. Their return would have been more like −1.74%!

Fortunately, not all investment practitioners conducted themselves in this manner. The true financial planning professional would not have needed a crystal ball to steer his or her clients to much happier results. An enlightened do-it-yourself planner-investor might have experienced better results as well. The secret rests in the discipline which can only be found through careful and thorough planning, the discipline that depends on truly understanding that a market segment which *over* performs will soon *under*perform, the discipline to stick to your strategy even when the markets make it uncomfortable.

The simple truth is that if you ask financial *salesmen,* they will tell you that 1999 was a great year, ripe with easy sales and fat commissions. However, if you ask a true financial *advisor,* he or she will reflect on a *very difficult* year, during which late nights and uncomfortable conversations with investors became standard fare, but also a year which ultimately solidified their relationship with loyal clients. You see, by 1999 most good planners had already been talking clients off the stock market ledge for two or three years, and could offer no proof that the year 2000 would not provide yet another banner stock market return.

It is indeed a time-consuming and patience-testing proposition to try to persuade sound-bite-bombarded investors that they should sell the fund that has averaged 31.4% and use the money to buy one which has averaged only 5.9%! This is especially true when one has been beating that same drum for several years in a row. Yet it is those extreme moments in which portfolios will either come in for a safe landing or fall apart in a fiery crash. During these periods there is no chart to which one can point and no proof that simple rebalancing will prove appropriate. In fact, as indicated by our example, in 1999 the rearview-looking charts all suggested that investors should simply buy stocks and watch them skyrocket. Yet, history tells us that the proceeding decade turned out to be one of the worst on record for stock investors.

The actual application of asset allocation and rebalancing is, of course, somewhat more complicated than has been presented here. A thorough understanding of asset classes and their interrelationship is required. In addition, competent professionals don't always agree about when and how often account rebalancing should be executed. Some portfolio managers reallocate annually, quarterly, or based on market-driven events. Best results are usually accomplished by those who develop a consistent strategy and stick with it. (For more about asset allocation visit the federal government's Guide to Asset Allocation at www.sec.gov/investor/pubs /assetallocation.htm. The use of asset allocation does not guarantee against loss.)

9

What about Cash, Bonds, and Stocks?

OST OF US don't need to become investment experts. Nevertheless, basic financial literacy is indispensable for anyone planning for retirement. Let us begin by identifying and distinguishing among the fundamental investment categories: cash, bonds, and equities.

Cash

To most of us most of the time, "cash" means dollar bills and metal coins. To investors it means savings and investing vehicles such as bank certificates of deposit, mutual fund money-market accounts, certain annuity contracts, and other principal guaranteed savings vehicles. The key trait of this investment category is liquid or easily accessible principal and that some may even be backed by some type of guarantee. Those guarantees may involve the Federal Deposit Insurance Corporation (FDIC), various state insurance arrangements, private insurance arrangements, or the assets of the issuer. Investors who intend to rely heavily on cash investments should make sure they know who or what is guaranteeing their investments. Even if your assets are backed by a guarantee, it still makes sense to maintain a healthy diversification in your portfolio. During the recession of 2008–2009, many banks, insurers, and money-market funds failed to live up to their promised guarantees. As a result, a taxpayer-funded bail out was created in part to protect average investors from potentially cataclysmic losses. The emergency program, along with other efforts, provided a federal guarantee designed to backstop investor assets held by struggling financial institutions. While cash investments typically have guaranteed principal, they generally do not have guaranteed interest payments; instead, the interest paid will generally fluctuate with prevailing economic conditions. While it may be possible to temporarily lock in a rate, such as for a long-term CD, the rate will change at the end of the term, and investors may have to forgo access to their money during the period or face a penalty. Guaranteed principal is a major attraction of these investments, but because the guarantee generally involves a middleman who is absorbing market risk on the investor's behalf, the rewards received over time typically have been less than those yielded by other investment types.

Debt

Debt, the second basic investment type, involves an investor making a loan as an investment; it also encompasses other, less familiar arrangements. Most people are familiar with the term *bond,* but many do not realize that a bond is little more than a formal agreement between the investor (lender) and the borrower (which may be a corporation, government, or other entity). Since the purpose of this work is to foster a broad understanding of investing and planning concepts, not to create investment experts, we will limit our debt discussion to bonds, which are by far the most common form of debt investing. Corporate bonds contain elements of both interest-rate risk and credit risk.

When buying bonds, savers need to be aware of three key ingredients. A bond agreement generally contains the principal loan amount, the duration or date at which the loan will be repaid (by the corporation or government and to the investor), and the coupon or interest rate. The coupon rate is generally paid monthly, quarterly, or annually and is the reward for lending the money. It may seem counterintuitive, but the best bond is not necessarily the one that pays the highest coupon rate. **One of the primary determinants of coupon rate is the creditworthiness of the bond issuer (borrower).** Creditworthiness indicates how likely the bond issuer is to pay the promised interest and return the borrowed money on the date of maturity. This is a very significant factor, and responsible money management therefore generally dictates that one not necessarily choose the highest-yielding bond.

A secondary consideration involves the length of indebtedness, with longer-maturity bond issues generally paying more interest than similarly creditworthy notes with a shorter duration. The longer an issuer plans to tie up your money, the more you should expect to be paid. The chart opposite details the general order of bond yields, which are based almost solely on the perceived ability of the issuer to repay principal and interest.

Lowest yield, highest credit quality

Municipal bonds

U.S. government bonds

AAA corporate bonds

Below AAA corporate bonds

Highest yield, lowest credit quality

Careful observers might notice that in this chart municipal bonds rank above U.S. government issues. This is due to their lower yields, not higher creditworthiness. While the U.S. federal government is currently considered the safest credit risk on the planet, many municipal bonds have periodically been able to get away with paying lower yields due solely to their tax-free status for many investors. Please remember that government bonds are only guaranteed as to timely payments of interest and principal and do not eliminate the previously mentioned market risk.

There are other considerations that can have a very significant impact on the bondholder (that would be you). Some bonds have a **call feature**, which means that the issuer maintains the right to buy back the bond before it reaches total maturity. The issuer of a callable bond is very unlikely to exercise its option if it favors the bondholder; therefore, buyers of callable bonds should expect higher compensatory yields than those associated with similar non-callable issues.

The final common feature we will cover is the **convertible clause.** A bond conversion clause allows the bondholder (you) to convert the bond into shares of the issuing company's stock. This is a good thing for investors, so bonds with a conversion feature will generally pay less than their counterparts with no such option. Consequently, the bond tradeoff is that while bonds do offer guaranteed interest and principal, the investor is required to hold the bond until maturity, which can be as long as 30 years. Bondholders wishing to cash in their bonds before maturity have to resort to selling them on the open market, which might gain them more or less than the original principal amount (this is called market risk). As a result, unlike with cash assets, bond investors may over the short term experience a meaningful loss of value. Accordingly, bond issuers have been forced to compensate investors with somewhat higher interest payments than can historically be found with cash assets.

IMPORTANT

The purchase of bonds is subject to availability and market conditions. Generally, the bond market is volatile; bond prices rise when interest rates fall and vice versa. Market risk is a consideration if bonds are sold or redeemed prior to maturity. Some bonds have call features that may affect income. Corporate bonds contain elements of both interest-rate risk and credit risk. Government bonds are guaranteed only as to timely payment of principal and interest and do not eliminate market risk.

Equity

The final investment category that we will consider is equity, or ownership positions. While most think of owning corporate stocks as holding equity, equity ownership can also entail real estate, currency, commodities, and a number of other less obvious assets. In contrast to the other investment or asset categories, equity ownership offers no guarantees. Therefore, while most cash-like investments provide guarantees of principal and bonds provide guarantees of income, ownership investments guarantee neither. To best understand the role of ownership in an investing society, we can look to the real-life analogy of home ownership. Although there is no guarantee that home buyers will be able to sell their homes for more than they paid for them, and in the short run, many may actually owe more than their home is worth, over time most homeowners experience meaningful growth in their homestead. In fact, with the possible exception of stock ownership, my experience is that most homeowners have admitted that, over time, their guaranteed investments proved considerably less financially rewarding than homeownership.

Our discussion of ownership assets will focus primarily on stock investing, especially diversified stock investing. For the vast majority of average Americans, the 401k (or 403b if you work for a nonprofit organization) provides an initial entree to equity investing. For responsible savers, the tax-deferred employer-sponsored plan may be rivaled only by homeownership for meaningful long-term wealth building. There exists a dual benefit for both types of investing as both venues have proven to garner significant long-term compounded rates of investment return (as compared to other categories) and incorporate structural investor discipline, which we will cover more fully in another chapter. The pros and cons of equity investing can be summarized as follows: Equities provide no guarantees and therefore are considered riskier than cash or debt (bond) investments. However, when long-term goals are taken into account, the higher investment rates of return often associated with equity ownership can actually reduce the risk of not saving enough money.

So what is a stock, and how does it generate growth for the investor? A stock is an ownership share in a publicly traded company. Because they hold stock, investors have the right to enjoy their share of company profit in the form of dividend payments and also their fair share of any core growth.[5] A good example of core growth might be a restaurant chain that continues to build more restaurants; your shares also represent ownership in the new locations and, therefore, are worth more to other investors. Shareholders have the potential to get the benefit of capital gains when they sell their shares to other investors, who hopefully pay more than the original purchase price. Because capital gains are dependent on the whims and emotions of a hypothetical or future buyer, the pricing can and often does swing wildly over very short periods of time. This short-term price reassessment represents the primary risk for investors with a well-diversified equity portfolio. Take a moment to consider the simple comparison shown at the top of the opposite page.

Let us take a moment to expand upon our earlier hypothetical example, in which we compared cash and bond investments for a couple who had amassed a $500,000 portfolio.

Investment Type	Trait	Common Uses
Cash	Guaranteed principal	Short- to medium-term savings, asset allocation
Debt (bonds)	Guaranteed income	Current income, medium- to long-term savings
Equity (stocks)	No guarantee	Long-term wealth building

Now assume that the couple is young and is still *planning* to amass a $500,000 portfolio. For the sake of this discussion, we will not take taxes or inflation into account, although in real life we certainly would. Our young couple plans to retire in 30 years, and, after careful consideration, decides to dutifully invest $300 per month, an amount that on their starting salaries requires considerable sacrifice. If invested in cash assets, which have a guaranteed principal, the account would likely only grow to around $220,000, assuming historical growth rates for the category. Conversely, bond investments, again assuming historical returns and an identical time horizon, would do better, but still fall short at a little over $300,000. Ultimately, only equity investments, with their associated higher historical long-term growth rates, would gain our couple the nest egg they need to realize their retirement dreams. **Therefore, we can conclude that although ownership (stock) investing exposes participants to significant and unshielded short-term risks, this type of asset can simultaneously help alleviate certain long-term challenges.**

This discussion, however, taking place as it does in the intellectual safety of a hypothetical realm, fails to address **the single most significant factor in investing: investor behavior (or misbehavior as the case may be). In the real world, savers** who invest for long-term goals frequently abandon appropriate disciplined approaches due to short-term temptations. In our next chapter, we will address this dangerous phenomenon and discover how you can improve your chances of sidestepping this common quagmire.

10

Investor Behavior

Numerous studies conducted over the years have all come to the same harsh conclusion: The vast majority of investors dramatically underperform the various markets in which they are invested. The key word here is "dramatically." We are not talking about a slight performance differential that can be explained away by fees or other easily identifiable variables. In fact, the performance discrepancy is often an enormous chasm rather than a minor fissure. Ask any professional financial advisor, and he or she will likely confirm that many prospective client interviews reveal that investors often have experienced negative returns (lost money) even during periods in which the investment markets themselves posted positive growth.

But how can this be? More important, what are the ramifications? Let us begin by addressing the latter. As discussed earlier, the traditional safety nets on which generations have come to rely are beginning to sag under the great pressures associated with modern longevity. With the near-total collapse of pensions and the soon-to-be-felt stress on Social Security,

Americans are being called upon to build and manage their own retirement nest eggs.

Unfortunately for Americans, most attempts to discuss the state of Social Security have immediately been trampled by a herd of political grandstanders. According to the annual report by Social Security trustees, which can be found at http://ssa-custhelp.ssa.gov/app/answers /detail/a_id/210 or by visiting the RetirementQuest.com site and accessing the link found on the Tool Box page, by 2035 payroll taxes will only be sufficient to cover about 50% of the program's costs, that is, the benefit payments to recipients. By 2080, when our children or grandchildren would be collecting benefits, tax revenues will only be sufficient to cover about 30% of outlays!

Even worse, since the mid-1980s, the popular program has generated trillions of dollars in "excess revenues"—in other words, more than was necessary to pay for promised benefits. Incredibly, although the goal was to hold the revenues in trust to fund the pending baby-boomer-induced shortfalls, the money has actually been simply spent by our government. According to the trustees, debate exists as to whether or not the trust fund is valid. According to proponents, the fund contains the implicit guarantee of the U.S. Treasury, making it as good as cash. Detractors argue that this amounts to nothing more than the federal government's IOU to itself; they point out that spending the trust fund to pay promised benefits (its purpose) will require additional dollar-for-dollar borrowing. Sadly, this looming reality has not been factored into federal budget forecasts since, officially speaking, the trust fund is valid and available to pay benefits.

While most people are at least somewhat aware of these issues, few know that according to law, once the trust fund is exhausted—it is anticipated that this will occur around the year 2030—the benefit formula is to be rewritten based upon the economics of the program at that time. **In simple terms, this means that we should expect, if all goes well, that around the year 2030 we will experience a benefit cut of about 50%.**

This task is formidable enough for the responsible and likely insurmountable for the less than responsible. Not only must we, using our limited resources, build a portfolio capable of generating 30 or 40 years' worth of retirement income, but this portfolio must also accommodate the taxes, inflation, and unexpected emergencies that appear along the way. In order to rise to this challenge, we simply cannot afford to lose a large portion of our wealth to mistakes and mismanagement.

From our earlier examples, we saw the dramatic impact that portfolio rates of return (growth) could have on our planning efforts. **A rule of thumb that illustrates this concept is known as the "rule of 72."[6] According to this financial planning tenet, if you divide the number 72 by your investment growth rate, the result will be the approximate amount of years it will take your portfolio to double in value. For example, if you anticipate a 7% annual (compounded) rate of growth, then it would take about 10 years for your portfolio to double in size**

(72 ÷ 7 = 10). Therefore, an investor who is 35 years old and figures to retire at 65 might expect his or her $100,000 nest egg to double about three times, reaching the meaningful sum of $800,000. But if through common investor errors that same portfolio only achieves a 4% growth rate, then the portfolio will take 18.5 years to double. This means that it will only double about 1.6 times in 30 years, resulting in a paltry $332,000— unlikely to prove sufficient for most couples to retire on (72 ÷ 4 = 18.5).

What about couples who expect to retire in the next few years? Does the point remain valid? In fact, the importance of squeezing available yield out of investments may be even more critical for those who depend upon their investments for income. Most investors want to know how much income they can draw from their portfolio. A better way to understand the issue, however, is to ask another question: How much portfolio do I need to generate my targeted income? Again, if we simplify by ignoring taxes and inflation, we could conclude that a $1 million portfolio that yields 7% in interest and/or capital growth (we call this combined figure "total return") would generate a $70,000 annual income. However, a portfolio generating a 4% total return would have to be $1,750,000 to generate a similar income. Please note that this example is in no way meant to suggest that investors should expect a 7% annual rate of return. Timing, risk tolerance, market fluctuation, and other factors influence what it is reasonable to assume, so these assumptions should only be made after thorough planning.

In a world in which sound investing must become integral, how can we as a nation be so bad at it? It will likely not come as a surprise that there are several factors at work. Let us begin at the beginning. Mankind, from our inception, has struggled for survival. When we contemplate the time in which homo sapiens have roamed the earth, it becomes apparent that only very recently have we enjoyed anything resembling free time. Through prehistory and into the modern era, most of us spent most of our days in pursuit of survival, and as a result, our bodies became hardwired for the purpose. Whether hunting a woolly mammoth or investing in dot-com stocks, we share an ingrained propensity to endlessly vacillate between greed and fear. In the past there were obvious advantages to jumping clear of an ill-tempered beast and then fighting for a fair share of the kill, but for a modern-day investor, these urges prove less than helpful.

Even for the most disciplined and intuitively aware investors, those primal urges have a way of surfacing at exactly the wrong moment. What else could explain the dot-com debacle, flipping condos, or overloading on bank stocks, if not that ancient instinct to fight for a share of the kill? While it is true that any single event can be explained by the news of the moment, the endless cycle of repetition suggests a deeper cause. Studies of the mutual fund industry, which provides an excellent indicator of investor sentiment, revealed that the largest inflows into stock-based mutual funds inevitably occur sometime within the few months leading up to a market crash. In fact, the largest stock-based fund flows ever recorded (as of 2002) were during the latter part of 1999 and early 2000, just weeks before the "new economy" imploded, dragging the stock market with it.[7] Similarly, we witnessed the largest retail investment flows into the real estate sector just prior to the recent multiyear collapse. In addition, retail oil investments peaked with a barrel selling for around $150—just before the price dropped to under $30, and of course it seemed no stocks were more popular than those in the banking sector during the period just prior to the bailout fiasco.

Lying beneath the surface we discern another common source of investor woe. Modern sound-bite media, delivered in a 24-hour-a-day nonstop fashion, inadvertently fans the flames of investor misbehavior. In reality, few will take the necessary time to garner an in-depth understanding of the multitude of facts and circumstances which surround the typical investment-related sound bite. Without this understanding, it is difficult to discern the important fact from the sales pitch. Perhaps more dangerously it is nearly impossible to turn off the information flow. Who among us can say that they were not aware while the tech bubble was brewing, or that oil had skyrocketed after the series of horrific events of 9/11, the war on terror, and Hurricane Katrina? Of course, few knew these were bubbles until they burst, and so were commonly portrayed as great investment opportunities that were not to be missed.

In their defense, the job of the media is to report the news of the day, and investor mania certainly qualifies.

If greed is the most dangerous of investor emotions, fear is its frequent companion. While the year 1999 experienced the largest retail stock fund inflows, 2002 experienced the largest outflows (which were eclipsed only by the panic selling in spring of 2009).[8] By that point in the economic cycle, the damage had already been done. Cashing out did not prevent many additional losses, yet that is what most people did. As a result, they did not participate in the ensuing rallies, which proved to be among the strongest on record. Most financial advisors who have been working with clients for a significant amount of time will confirm that within weeks or even days of a market peak they are inundated with phone calls from clients demanding to purchase stock, and that a similar flood of "cash-me-out" requests occurs immediately prior to a market turnaround. An advisor's reaction to those calls speaks volumes about his or her character and level of competence.

This brings us to another culprit in encouraging investor misbehavior; a general lack of understanding about what causes stocks and bonds to experience those drastic price swings. Our discussion will not include commodities (precious metals, oil, soy beans, etc.) since they are frequently affected by less predictable variables and so are best left for the exceptionally savvy.

The two primary factors driving stock prices are intrinsic value and speculative pressures. Almost any profitable company has some value, even if it is only the sum of its plants, equipment, and cash on the balance sheet. Realistically, however, the intrinsic value of a company, although not always accurately reflected in its stock price, also includes a reasonable estimate of future profits. This measure of worth tends to focus on the long term, so it does not usually change with the same ferocity as stock prices. The day-to-day, often celebrated and sometimes lamented, movements of stock prices are driven primarily by short-term trading decisions. These often create vast discrepancies between intrinsic company value and the momentary selling price of the stock. Traders are not so concerned about the long-term profit picture of a company as they are about the price someone is willing to pay over the next few weeks, days, or even seconds. Professional traders have generally acted upon data well before it becomes a media sound bite. When the data is significant enough, a domino-like chain reaction kicks into full swing with round-the-clock news coverage, brokers inciting their clients to react, and a host of other previously mentioned influences. The tsunami which ensues has a way of taking all reason with it. If it is a downward spiral, then asset prices tend to settle somewhere far below their fair intrinsic value. If it is an upward-bound crescendo, then prices tend to peak well above anything reasonable. Here is where mistakes are made: investors who have long-term goals (more than ten years) react, for all the reasons mentioned earlier in this chapter, to the short-term hysteria.

The final wellspring of investor error which we will cover is that of the investment industry itself. As a longtime CERTIFIED FINANCIAL PLANNER™ practitioner, I have come to the unavoidable conclusion that the financial services industry is in many cases quite culpable in the regrettably poor performance of the average investor. I am not thinking primarily of fees or fraud. While fees are an issue, the competitive marketplace has proven quite successful in generating a decade or more of downward pressure on pricing. Nevertheless, prudent investors should educate themselves regarding the specific costs and benefits of working with an advisor. When it is exposed, fraud is highly visible and often horrific in its impact on the lives of those affected, but it is nonetheless rare. While not foolproof, an excellent rule of thumb for investors is to simply never write anyone a check. It is clearly unlawful for registered brokers to accept client funds directly into their own account *for any reason*. Moreover, the registration process, continuing education, and ever-present industry oversight renders it implausible that anyone in the profession would be unaware of this restriction.[9] This consideration should also apply to companies or partnerships controlled by an advisor. While in some cases it is legal for a Registered Investment Advisor firm to accept direct client funds, most reputable ones will instruct investors to make checks out to a third-party custodian. (It is generally permissible, however, for Registered Investment Advisor firms to accept client funds which merely represent payment of earned fees.) A primary role of the custodian is to help safeguard your money from fraud. Also, the custodian should ideally be a member of the Security Investors Protection Corporation (SIPC), which guards against failure of the custodian.

The modern financial services industry dates back to the early stages of the Industrial Revolution. During this period, investments were not intended for the average person. The thinking went something like this: Only the wealthy have enough money to actually invest anything, and they can afford to lose money; if they lose money, they will probably still be rich. Services were offered almost exclusively through a small number of brokerage firms as well as an insurance company or two. It was largely assumed that if a person had money to invest they were also savvy. As a result, and in a sign of the times, the brokerage houses and insurance companies emerged as true selling cultures. No consultative, time-consuming, carefully deliberative process existed; the goal was to make a sale and move on. Now, do not get me wrong: most people who work for modern brokerage firms are hardworking, bright, well-intentioned individuals who have learned to treat their clients well. The problem is that many of the firms that employ them still foster the hard line sales approach. They accomplish this through sales quotas, incentives, and various forms of indoctrination.[10] The sales pitch goes something like this: "We are the best so buy our stuff." This approach inadvertently, or in some cases purposely, takes advantage of those primordial investor vulnerabilities.

Again, using the dot-com era as an example, we can see how poignantly this plays out. In the most extreme cases, certain firms, finding that they held dangerously large quantities of certain stocks, decided that motivating their sales force to push them onto their unsuspecting clients would be a convenient way to unload the inventory. The firms in question paraded corporate economists and other high-profile experts to convince their sales force (brokers) that the new economy and hence the dot-com shares would continue their exponential growth indefinitely and that if their clients were not involved they would miss out. Incentives were sometimes offered, including higher pay, corner offices, and lucrative trips, designed to encourage brokers to move the stuff fast. Too few brokers proved wise and courageous enough to buck the onslaught. Now let us add a phone ringing off the hook with media-manic customers demanding dot-com shares and a more complete picture emerges!

11

Choosing a Source of Advice

I T IS IN those moments when the stakes are highest and emotions running strongest that mistakes are made. That is when investors most need a consultative voice of reason, not a sales pitch. Consider the following allegory from the frenzied dot-com era.

An investor turns on the television, reads the newspaper, listens to the radio, and is inundated by images and messages about the dot-com millionaires. Their techno-investment prowess has earned them early retirements, Lear Jets, yachts, and other symbols of massive wealth attached to a visage barely able to support facial hair. Over Thanksgiving, our hypothetical saver listens to a brother-in-law touting his technology shares and how they went up in value by 3,000% since he last bragged (about two weeks before) about his superior investment acumen, really cool new boat, plans to quit work and trade online, all the while narrowly avoiding Freudian slips about the size of his enormous portfolio. Exhausted and frustrated, our responsible hero calls his investment guy for advice. What does his advisor say? Consider these two possibilities:

In scenario A, the advisor says, "Dot-com? What a great idea! Lucky you work with us because we are the best and can get stuff that nobody else has."

In scenario B, the advisor says, "A 3,000% rate of return? When we spent those four hours creating your financial plan, we discovered that you will likely be okay with a 7% return that is somewhat consistent. Are you sure that risking everything on an unproven high flyer is wise? Let's talk about the dot-com mania . . ."

What are the key differences between these approaches? In the first scenario, a quick and easy sale might have been made, but the outcome would almost certainly have been poor. In the second, it is likely that a long conversation ensued, during which no sale was made but the investor learned enough to draw a far wiser conclusion.

What about discount brokers? Are they any better? Unfortunately, in my opinion, they have every appearance of being cast from the same mold as the traditional brokerages since their sales pitches appear dangerously similar: "Buy our stuff. We are better because we are cheaper." There are, of course, many circumstances in which the online discount brokers and no-load funds are quite appropriate, but like all else financial, it helps to get a fair presentation of the pros and cons. In the case of our hypothetical investor, I do not think it much matters if his brother-in-law paid $1,000 a trade for a full-service broker or $7 to a discount outfit; in either case his portfolio probably crashed when the dot-com bubble burst and he wound up on our hero's doorstep with an outstretched hand.

Responsible investing involves asking and answering the following question: What resources do you use to enable

wise decisions? The table below provides some insight into the relative appropriateness of the various financial services providers.

Discount broker or no-load fund	Main benefit is reduced cost, which can be significant over time. However, the discount arrangement typically leaves the investor bearing the full brunt of responsibility. Even the best trading tools and occasional anonymous phone conversation will not likely prevent common investor mistakes. This relationship is best suited to the do-it-yourself investor who looks forward to a lifetime of immersion in financial management. If this describes you, this book is probably just one of countless financial works in your library.
Full-service traditional broker	These service providers are historically transaction oriented, charging a one-time commission for a buy or sell transaction that may be as high as 5% or more. Investors looking to simply buy and hold and who want help with their decisions might be well served. Use caution, however, because a certain conflict of interest is inherent with this arrangement.
Fee-only investment advisor	As the name implies, the fee-only advisor does not charge a sales commission but an ongoing fee, often around 1% annually. The idea is to avoid conflicts of interest. The advisor has a single incentive, which is to keep clients happy and on board with the planning process.

When we take a bird's-eye view of the traditional sources of investment services, which include banks, full-service brokerage firms, discount brokers, insurance companies, and mutual fund companies, I feel a very confusing set of messages emerges, as shown in the table at the top of the next page.

Provider	Message
Discount brokers	If you pay for an advisor you are foolish because they are all lazy *and* stupid.
Mutual funds	Buy us because we are better than everyone else.
Full-service brokers	You are not capable of doing this yourself so you must hire us. Also, we are smarter than everyone else.
Insurance companies	Buy our stuff because it is the best, and we have the coolest animated mascot.

Considering the enormous gravity of investment decisions to the retirement planning arena, and the cost of failure both at an individual level and, even more frightening, for the nation, a clear imperative emerges. **It is time for the investment services industry to *grow up* and begin to provide the holistic help that Americans require.** Rather than finger pointing and chest pounding, it would be far more appropriate for industry players to encourage and assist people in finding the services that best suit them. In reality, there are plenty of customers available to support a robust industry without trying to convince legitimate do-it-yourself investors that they must hire an advisor or suggesting that someone who values and is willing to pay for good advice is somehow a sucker.

There is some light at the end of the tunnel. The independent registered investment advisor model comes much closer to achieving objectivity than many of the alternatives, since the independents often have no product to sell except advice. What's more, the unprecedented rise of the independent model has drawn the attention of the big traditional firms, who are for the most part trying to emulate the script. While many of the big firms are having difficulty severing their ties to the past, certain of their branch offices are doing excellent work. So if you're looking for an advisor, how do you tell if the one you're considering is a good one?

Here are some guidelines based on my many years in the retirement planning business. Ask prospective advisors how they get paid. While a practitioner who earns sales commissions is not necessarily up to no good, this arrangement does impose a certain pressure to repeatedly make sales. A commission is a one-time, up-front payment of usually around 5–6% of the amount invested. Conversely, the typical fee-only planner might charge a 1% pay-as-you-go fee, generally based upon the assets upon which they advise or even a flat one time planning fee. This encourages a very different relationship since, to earn the same amount of money, the planner has to keep you as a happy client for five or six years, whereas the commission salesperson only has to keep you happy long enough to sign the paperwork. This does not mean that the commission broker will ignore you after the sale is made; he or she just has no *incentive* except to try to sell you something else later on. There is some regulatory precedent here as well since (as of this writing) the commissioned broker is only held accountable for investment suitability at the *time of sale*, but the registered investment advisory firm functioning in an ongoing fee agreement is required to ensure suitability on an *ongoing* basis (fiduciary standard).

Another common source of conflict of interest involves the use of captive funds. These products are created and managed by the firm which employs the broker or representative. If the funds recommended also have the same brand name that is on your advice giver's business card, it is almost certainly a captive arrangement. If this is the case, the salesperson is likely to have additional incentives or even requirements to sell those specific investments. Again, this does not necessarily indicate that the funds are poor performers; it just suggests that questions may exist regarding the seller's objectivity and ability to judge whether these products are suitable for you.

The vast majority of advisors and planners that I have met are decent folks who are deeply concerned about the welfare of their clients. The general shortcomings of industry leadership do not necessarily apply to your personal planner. Nevertheless, taking the above criteria into account will help you choose the right advisor for you.

When we consider the role of sales pitches combined with that of sound-bite nonstop media, the plethora of often conflicting information dictates that responsible planning incorporate a strategy for information dissemination. This is one of the areas in which the calm, patient, discipline of an experienced advisor can be a real asset. If during times of tumult, your source of advice (professional or otherwise) recommends panicked reaction, it is probably a good idea to find a new one. Nevertheless, you will be most tempted to ignore the gentle suasions of your advice giver at exactly the wrong moment in time. Remember dot-com, oil, and bank stocks. **Therefore, the tenets of good guidance generally should include timely availability, conflict-free opinions, interactive dialogue, and excellent overall communication skills.** Those who seek the advice of a professional may wish to use this as a template for evaluating providers.

Those who wish to develop and execute their own financial planning strategies will find that their efforts to systematically make sense of the flood of information will prove a key challenge and as such warrant considerable attention. For do-it-yourself investors (similar to the professional advisor), the pursuit of reliable sources of good information should be thought of as a wise, yet endless preoccupation.

12

The Market Cycle

I N AN INDUSTRIAL-LEANING mercantile culture, perhaps nothing exerts broader influence than the economic cycle. The periodic vacillations of economic activity have created and undone public policy, replaced regimes, made fortunes, won world wars, employed millions, built lives—and destroyed them. Most germane to this book, however, is the market cycle's history of moving massive amounts of money from error-prone investors to the market-savvy. **Those planning for retirement need to be aware of two essential market facts: When the economy expands it will eventually contract, and when it contracts it will inevitably rise again.**

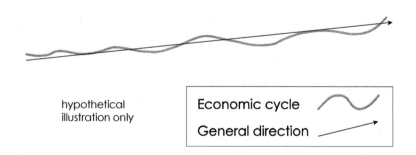

hypothetical
illustration only

Economic cycle	
General direction	

As we can see, while there are occasional setbacks, the general trend has been up. In the industrial age, the average length of each segment of this cycle has been about seven years from peak to peak or trough to trough, with some notable variations. As a result, "long-term" is often taken to mean about ten years or more. As the graphic suggests, the rate of expansion and contraction in the U.S. has generally fallen within a fairly narrow range. Between 1980 and 2010 the U.S. economy only contracted by more than 5% on three occasions and never expanded by more than 10% in any annual period. A review of fluctuations occurring prior to the 1980s, or a comparison with still-developing nations, will indicate variability greatly in excess of that of the modern U.S. The primary reasons for the comparatively tame experience of the previous 30 years are government action, a greater understanding of the market cycle by business and industry leaders, and improvements in technology. The purpose of this book is not to delve deeply into how these mechanisms function, but merely to point out that we have enjoyed a period of relative economic calm (although not necessarily stock market calm). One chief cause of the meltdown of 2008 and 2009 was a widespread (although perhaps temporary) reassessment of the actual abilities of the above players to maintain this level of stability. It would be appropriate at this point to ask the following question: If the economy has only vacillated within a relatively narrow range, then why have my investments swung so severely? The hypothetical graphic at the top of the next page compares the economic cycle with the equity investment markets.

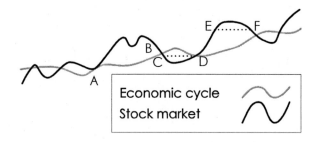

A casual observation will quickly reveal that the gyrations of the stock market (black), while ultimately dependent upon the economic cycle (gray), nevertheless swing with significantly increased vigor. Recent history clearly backs up this data because during the same period, since 1980, the economy as measured by GDP has basically held within a range of positive 10% and negative (–) 5% annually, while investor account balances have experienced volatility in excess of 50%![11] In keeping, the recent market implosion and economic cataclysm of 2008–2009, dubbed the "great recession," witnessed an economic swing from 3% *growth* in 2006 to a 3.8% *decline* in mid-2009. An economic swing of less than 7% from peak to trough resulted in a stock market collapse in which investors lost on average 55% or more of their equity holdings, the reins of political power changed hands, and a host of iconic institutions were laid to waste.

So why do company stock prices, linked as they are to the general economy, generate a roller-coaster-like experience while comparatively the economy itself is generally more akin to a kiddie ride? The answer is investor emotion. Drawing from our discussion on investor behavior, let's review what shareholders are experiencing during an economic contraction and market decline.

When I explain this scenario to clients or during speaking engagements, I often use the analogy of driving a car. Cruising along with your eyes on the road ahead, you pass a shocking accident complete with flashing lights and warning flares. (Referring to the chart on the previous page, you will see that the stock market has generally begun a decline before anyone has noticed the car wreck [B–C] of economic activity [the collapse of subprime mortgages in the most recent installment].) **Nervous, and a bit curious, you adjust the rearview mirror to get a better look at what happened. By taking your eyes off the road ahead, you have just increased your chance of having a wreck of your own.** In the mirror you see that the accident is a bad one, involving blood, smashed metal, and broken glass. On the radio, the tragedy is being covered by all of the major stations. Inexplicably drawn and yet queasy about the outcome, you listen intently to the reports and adjust the mirror again for an even better look. The worse the accident, the more media coverage it receives and the more intently you focus on the carnage. Soon you are driving down the road, eyes fixated on the rearview mirror, mind focused on what happened in the recent past, and radio bleating out the nauseating details. At this point most are no longer thinking about what lies ahead and are only able to react to the emotion of the moment. As long as the road stays perfectly straight, you can carry on this way for some time. Unfortunately, the road always turns and when it does you may speed right off it. Again glancing at the previous chart, you will notice that the stock market has generally begun a recovery before the economy begins a rebound. Unfortunately, when it does, most investors (reacting to the emotional memory of carnage) have sold their shares and so miss out on the ensuing rally (C–D on page 97).

Staying with our most recent example (as of the writing of this book), we witnessed an astounding stock market recovery which began in early spring of 2009, even as the economy had yet to post its most dismal performance, even as the media reports were at their most grim, even as predictions were dismal, even as way too many salespeople were advising their customers to get out of the market and buy something else, and even as the largest *outflow* in the history of stock-based mutual funds was well underway. **The moral of the story is: Keep your eyes on the road and you may be in much better shape when the curves arrive.**

What does the rearview mirror look like for the average investor? During periods of economic and market growth, things will look pretty good (line segment A–B on page 97). Investment accounts routinely post positive gains, the evening news regularly reports that all is well, and the ever-present armies of salespeople will be pushing times-are-good products, touting high rates of return and sure-bet outcomes. As the expansion continues, the rhetoric heats up, adding to the sense that all must be well. By the late stages of expansion, those reluctant investors who are always slow to get in jump on board with both feet. Their dollars, entering the market, amplify the fervor; appearing to confirm that the rearview looks pretty good, and seducing us into thinking it will surely continue. Notice line segment E-F on page 97: during these periods things look best in the mirror, but they actually prove to be poor times to commit money to the market.

Manufacturers, drinking the same Kool-Aid, ramp up production because things *feel* so good. With demand high (as it inevitably is when account balances are up and the media confirms that all is well), managers come to believe that their greatest risk is not making enough *stuff*. They theorize that market share will be lost to competitors if they don't have enough inventories to satisfy the insatiable demand. Factories kick into overtime, warehouses swell with goods, and payrolls explode. All looks good, especially in the rearview mirror. At some point, however, some variable, always unexpected, causes a pause in the fast pace of consumption. During the most recent market gyration, cutbacks by overextended homeowners served as catalyst while unaware investors, homeowners, and business leaders sped headfirst into the impending disaster. Even the slightest pause in demand, when it occurs during a period of heightened manufacturing activity, will quickly cause inventories to swell and will inescapably lead to production cutbacks. It is impossible to predict the precise catalyst or moment that these directional changes will come about, yet they *always* have done so.

Business, faced with mounting stores of unsold *stuff,* cuts back on production, and these cutbacks in turn send ripples through the entire economy. The media catches on and confirms that things don't look so good. At this point we should also consider the role of politics in the equation. In recent memory, whichever party is out of office has seized on the opportunity to declare that the current state of affairs is *the worst ever* and certainly the fault of the *incumbent party*. In an unfathomable show of poor leadership, enormous amounts of money are poured into spreading such propaganda, which serves (even if unintentionally) to further exacerbate an already bleak situation.

Allow me here to say a word about market timing, a trading technique in which guesses are made about future market movements. As we discuss the inevitability of expansion turning to contraction and vice versa, *timing* would appear to be a wise strategy. However, this book is in no way intended to support the notion of market timing. Delving into the micro-details of timing is beyond the scope of this work; it suffices to say that the vast majority of market-timing strategies *do not work*. While *all* sound good in theory, and *all* work historically and on paper, they uniformly make the implausible assumptions that investors will always act in the future as they have in the past and that they will do so at the same predictable point in time. I believe both of these assumptions have proven flawed. **Furthermore, as we have discussed in other chapters, strategies designed to beat the market must by design carry increased risks, whereas the goal of solid financial planning should be to reduce both risk and uncertainty.**

So if we cannot predict the timing of a market cycle, how do we know that the tide does always turn? Simply put, because we must consume. While we might buy more or less during a given period, and while the duration of those phases may (and will) vary—buy we must. As the economy begins a downward slope and the rearview takes on a very different appearance, we are nevertheless forced to buy. For example, during the downturn of 2008–2009, the auto industry was particularly hard-hit. For a host of reasons consumers cut back on big-ticket items and financing was difficult to come by. Auto sales ground to a near halt. But that state of affairs could only continue if the average car or truck lasted over 30 years! In 2009 approximately 11 million automobiles were sold in the U.S., but about 14.5 million were sent to the junk yard that same year.[12] Similarly, the slow rate of home sales could only continue if Americans held on to their dwellings for over a hundred years. These assumptions are, of course, quite implausible. Therefore, just as the frenzied activity which occurs during a period of economic expansion cannot be sustained indefinitely, neither can the lethargic pace associated with contraction.

While politics plays a role in the economy, it is perhaps different from that which is frequently assigned by the average pundit, who seems to assume that public policy is a chief cause of economic activity. In the short term, the constant ebb and flow of the economic tide generally overpowers policy. Expansions and contractions occur regardless of the gyrations of lawmakers and executive branches. Regarding a peak-to-peak economic cycle, short of assailing the very framework of our society, the most that a government can typically hope to accomplish is to shorten the periods of contraction, lessen their severity, or perhaps prolong a growth phase. If politicians are lucky, their tenure will coincide with an expansion period and thus they will surely get credit for it. If they are not so fortunate, their term in office will occur during a time of contraction and they will almost certainly pay the price at the polls. In fact, studies have determined that in almost every case during the last century, the bulk of government stimulus rescue efforts did not actually work their way into the economy until after the targeted recession was already over!

However, government policy can have a powerful *cumulative* effect on the economy over long periods. Consider the presidency of George W. Bush. From a purely economic standpoint, he was handed an economy which, after nearly twenty years of almost unchecked expansion, was set for a cyclical recoil. Contrary to the opinion of some, I do not believe his policies brought about the dot-com collapse or the sluggish economy which ensued. In fact, the recession of 2002 was mild when all factors were considered, and this could well be lauded as an accomplishment of the administration. The primary mistake of the Bush policies was the rampant overspending which sowed the seeds of longer-term economic headwinds in the form of federal debt.

Diversified economies, like those which are required to serve vast populations, have flourished with the following ingredients: entrepreneurial risk taking, access to capital for business building purposes, raw materials, and a highly motivated (and educated) workforce. **The reckless trend of political leadership to continually pander for votes by promising ever-increasing benefits while refusing to pay for them represents the single most significant threat to our economy (and way of life) over the long term.** As a nation, we have already reached the critical tipping point and will soon have to face the choice of cutting massive entitlement programs **or** raising taxes to cover the gaping deficit—and we cannot simply raise the taxes. When the current (year 2010) $14 trillion federal debt is considered along with the interest payments due on said obligations and the enormity of future mandates like Social Security and Medicare, any attempt to raise the unfathomable amount of taxes needed would have the effect of *killing the golden goose*. A tax tsunami of this proportion would severely reduce the amount of investible capital, crush entrepreneurial risk taking, and demotivate our workforce.

Entrepreneurial Risk Taking: The Key to Job Growth

The interplay between entrepreneurial risk taking and the availability of investment capital provides the engine of job creation, economic activity, sustainability of our culture, and the tax base upon which all government programs depend. Let's take a moment to consider what is required to set these mechanisms in motion.

The vast majority of jobs in the U.S. come from small and midsized businesses, which account for over 70% of all employment in our country.[13] But what does it take for an entrepreneur to create jobs?

Most small businesses are begun by those who have strong technical skills and/or advanced education. In short, they are also very employable individuals. Therefore, many are forced to make a choice between holding a dependable and often well-paying job with an established organization, or to risk their benefits and income to launch a new endeavor. It takes a special type of person endowed with courage, vision, and organizational skills to enter and successfully navigate the treacherous and competitive waters of the business world. In fact, about half of all businesses fail within their first two years of existence.

Heroic attributes alone are not enough. Entrepreneurs also require investment capital to open offices, pay salaries, stock inventory, and so on. When we add a skilled and educated workforce, a more complete picture emerges of what is required for job creation. Skyrocketing tax rates have the effect of both reducing available capital *and* smothering entrepreneurial risk taking by targeting those profits which serve as the incentive. In future chapters we will discuss how the 401k plan carries the potential to merge the interests of business owners and their employees, and to provide a ready supply of capital, likely providing a ray of hope in an otherwise frightening economic forecast.

In typical form, 2009's health-care spending proposal was pitched as *paid for.* Yet on closer inspection we saw that the proposed $500 billion–plus price tag was to be funded largely through Medicare savings—Medicare already runs an annual shortfall of $570 billion, and that figure is predicted to swell to a trillion dollars annually in the coming decade![14] Unfortunately, the overwhelming effect of these deficit numbers renders tax increases both inevitable and insufficient to solve the fundamental problem. If our government were to attempt to raise enough taxes to pay our way out of the impending conundrum, the essential factors required for economic growth would simply be choked out of existence. History is replete with examples of political parties promising to replace personal responsibility and hard work with government-sponsored *free stuff.* The results are inexorably the same: collapse of the system. To be fair and balanced, lest it appear that I am picking on only one political party, the prior administration, in a classic case of vote pandering, added a mountain of costs to the same beleaguered Medicare program in the form of prescription drug benefits, which have since proven metaphorically to be the most addictive drugs of all. The addition of these benefits is a large part of the reason why the program is set to run a trillion-dollar annual shortfall in the coming decade.[15]

Furthermore, to illustrate the universally habit-forming nature of *free stuff*, in just a few short years the discussion about prescription drug coverage has completely shifted focus from "What will this do to our children's future?" to those few out-of-pocket cost items which remain! In fact, in 2010 the government issued $250 checks to benefit recipients to cover the so-called "doughnut hole." This is not meant to suggest that healthcare and prescriptions are not an essential aspect of responsible planning, because they are. I only suggest that responsibility requires that massively expensive programs be accompanied by honest cost-related dialogue.

There is hope, however. The one variable that historical models have lacked is a large and financially well prepared middle class. While it would be difficult to describe our current state of individual financial affairs in such glowing terms, we still have time in which to collectively make better decisions and thus impact the outcome. Recalling again the words of a wise and famed leader:

> "Ask not what your country can do for you—
> ask what you can do for your country."
>
> —JFK

What we can do for our country is to prepare ourselves financially, thus providing a social cushion for the challenges ahead. Prepare ourselves so that we might help our children out of the economic mess which our leaders seem recklessly intent on handing them. Prepare ourselves so that we might provide an example by which we can hold our elected officials accountable. In the coming chapters we will discuss how we got here, and the essential role which responsible decision making must play in our personal and collective future.

13

A Dark Pact on a Summer Day

HE PEOPLE OF the United States had little reason to trust Joseph Stalin. After all, the Soviets under his direction had openly sought the end of capitalism. His policies eliminated any functional political opposition by banning all parties except the Communist Party. Individual freedoms were trampled underfoot, and the media fell under singular government control. Totalitarians seized all manner of economic production. And then there were the purges: Stalin, a larger-than-life sadistic ideologue, for whom existing laws merely stood in the way of creed, sent millions to unimaginable fates.

While the main purpose for the purges was to eliminate political opposition, imagined or otherwise, a secondary goal was to terrify the cowed population into conforming to the Soviet version of economy. Choice was gone; someone else would decide occupation and location. Personal gain was out of the question; the rank and file would toil merely for the good of the society as determined by the dominant.

Meanwhile, on a German hillside not far away, a menace of a different form took root. Initially intrigued by the leadership of the fledgling National Socialist German Workers Party, a young Adolf Hitler joined the movement and soon began to reshape the party to reflect his own views. The maniacal belief in a superior race, coupled with an intense hatred of those deemed inferior, intertwined with the political party's desire to destroy the wealthy class through a series of doctrines that included the elimination of investment profits for individuals and other anti-capitalist measures. By 1933, hundreds of thousands of brown-shirted supporters goose-stepped down the streets of Berlin. Within weeks, new elections were announced. These mock contests were little more than a power grab accompanied by extreme violence and inhuman brutality. The collapse of democracy in the German state brought about the immediate suspension of all personal liberties. Educational institutions, the press, and a newly created secret police became full-time instruments of public manipulation.

Unfortunately for the rest of the world, Hitler proved a brilliant orator, inciting millions with a vision steeped in intolerance and aggression. Under his direction, the Nazis seized the personal property of their countrymen, enslaving and massacring the innocent on a scale previously unimaginable. From a Western perspective, perhaps the only redeeming quality attributed to the insufferable dictator was his ardent hatred for and distrust of Communism.

On August 23, 1939, the free world awoke to the shocking news that Hitler and Stalin had signed the Nazi-Soviet Non-Aggression Pact. The audacious Nazi state had annexed the Rhineland three years earlier, and with the Soviet deal now struck, the two armies swallowed up the sovereign state of Poland in a matter of months. Once-great nations such as France, Italy, Spain, Austria, Denmark, and others had either joined forces or been trampled under by seemingly unstoppable armies. Also under fire were Great Britain, the Middle East, and the continent of Africa.

Many in the United States viewed the conflict as a foreign matter and scoffed at the notion of joining in the mêlée. On December 7, 1941, at a place called Pearl Harbor, the myth of American isolation was bombed into oblivion. The conflict, to which the United States was now fully committed, extended to all oceans, the Asian continent, and all major U.S. territories.

The members of this generation, still scarred by vivid memories of a great depression that had inescapably permeated their lives, now dropped their hammers, stepped away from assembly lines, took off their ties, and enlisted in military services. **Imbued with a sense that all was not fine, they steeled themselves to make a difference, risking everything to shape the course of history**. The women of this greatest of generations, empowered by the image of Rosie the Riveter, joined the workforce, providing desperately needed materials of war. In the ultimate demonstration of personal responsibility, the men and women of our nation out-produced, out-supplied, and out-fought the forces of tyranny that threatened our shores.

The mushroom cloud that signaled the end of this epic struggle also touched off a challenge that would loom for decades. In spite of overcoming the greatest of threats, members of this generation would toil for the rest of their lives under a cloud of potential unspeakable devastation. There was no reason to assume that everything would simply be fine. Personal responsibility had become a way of life, to which they owed their very existence. They had done and sacrificed everything for the future of their beloved nation. Upon returning to industry, they brought with them their fears, dreams, courage, and perspective, creating the greatest economic machine the globe had ever witnessed.

This juggernaut of free enterprise built a world previously unknown. According to the U.S. Census Bureau, median household income in 1950 was $2,570 for the average male worker. By the year 2005, this figure stood at $30,500. Even after adjusting for inflation, personal income nearly doubled, and for women and minorities the increases were even more significant. With the rising tide of personal income, this austere age group rationed their wealth in preparation for a future about which they stubbornly remained leery.

The parents and grandparents of the baby boomers believed that responsibility best rested on individual shoulders; the personal savings rate in 1960 was 5.4%, quite an accomplishment considering that the personal income standard stood at about half of that which we enjoy today.[16] Peaking at 14.5% in 1975, the savings rate then dwindled to an astonishing −0.8% by 2008,[17] leaving the astute observer to wonder with alarm: How is it possible that this great nation of take-charge, self-reliant, responsibility seekers could possibly have become comfortable consistently spending more than they earned?

14

The Boomers

T HE BABY BOOMER generation made its grand entrance
onto a scene very different from the one that launched
their immediate predecessors. For most, Nazis were little
more than bad guys in cheap movies, and our image of
the Japanese warrior was derived largely from the bumbling
television sitcom *McHale's Navy*. Even the horrific reality that
was the nuclear-tipped Cold War, much like the fabled frog
in the pot of water, was reduced to a comfortable and familiar
environment in which millions spent their days. Starting from
the childhood age at which we first uttered the question "why,"
we were assured that "it could never really happen."Détente
guaranteed us that no button would ever really get pushed.
Who could blame our parents from shielding us from such an
apocalyptic state of affairs? To their credit, they believed this
to be a mess of their doing, and in their typical, responsible-
minded manner, they were determined to protect us from this
dread.

The boomer experience of war bore little resemblance
to that of their parents. In Korea, the stage was set for a three-

way conflict between meddling superpowers. For the first time since World War I, the U.S. was engaged in combat that raged nowhere near our shores. Even the most creative warmongers had to stretch their imaginations in order to portray the event as a direct threat to the existence of our great nation. From this conflict, set on the Chinese border, we also learned how to fight to, and then accept, an uncomfortable standoff. Far different from the previous win-at-all-cost approach to war, now the cost in lives and material would begin to play a predominant role in battlefield policy.

Like the "canary in a coal mine," the Vietnam War brought on a defining shift in the American psyche. Signaling the first signs of distress, the proverbial songbird, caged deep in the heartland of America, made a notable shift from one side of its cage to the other.

For the first time ever, the U.S. military lost a foreign war. Yet, remarkably, we at home would experience no sense of direct threat. We could lose a war, be vanquished from the battlefield, and still be okay. After all, the field of conflict was on the opposite side of the world. There was no direct threat to our shores, no torpedoes tearing into our commercial shipping, and no enemy aircraft carriers looming on the horizon.

This war, perhaps the central event of a generation, served as both a cause and a simultaneous indicator of change. Another American first was the fact that a significant portion of the general public blamed the average soldier for the policies of our leadership. GIs, many of whom were forced against their will to enter the fray, returned home, wounded physically and psychologically, to an environment that they were not expecting. Scorned, spat upon, lambasted, and eventually ignored, these servicemen received nothing resembling the hero's welcome they had expected and deserved, the welcome afforded every prior generation of foreign war veterans.

However, the imperceptible yet weighty shift on the part of the proverbial canary was not the *outcome* of the war or the throngs of impassioned protesters. The real shift was that for the first time since the World War II generation was dubbed "the greatest," *their offspring,* who until now had only experienced lives imbued with plenty, would flex their political muscle. Motivated by a new sense of idealism, the children of bounty held the promise for a new and better way. This flower-powered generation, unlike any before, coupled a life of material comfort with the experience that even war was not a threat to our great nation. They dared to dream of utopian fairness, the sharing of unlimited resources, and worldwide cooperation. While this mindset embodied a new sense of earthly grandeur (the aim of every fairy tale and the objective of most religions), it also contained a dangerous sense of naïveté. Even while most Americans appeared unable to see it, a reality so far from our own, people around the world were struggling for economic survival. In other countries, many of which were still reeling from the devastation wreaked by a world at war, the focus was on global competitiveness. The canary drew a sharp breath.

15

Born into Peace and Prosperity

THE BOOMER GENERATION arrived coincidentally with an American military for which supremacy had been firmly established; decades would pass before a challenge would be issued so close to our shores. Domestic factories, schools, and infrastructure had largely and singularly escaped the wide-scale destruction vested upon the rest of the world. Enjoying little competition, American entrepreneurialism exploded. For the 20-year period beginning in 1950, U.S. GDP (gross domestic product, a measure of economic activity) expanded by an average of 4.56% annually, compared to the 20 years that ended 2008, which recorded a 2.85% average.[18]

Most baby boomers can remember a time in which "Made in Japan" was synonymous with "junk." We rarely saw anything made anywhere other than in the United States or possibly Japan. The free world envied our culture. Considered the best by most, American-made movies, music, cigarettes, vehicles, and other manufactured goods made their way around the globe. Parents of the baby boomers, educated under the GI Bill, left universities and fueled an unprecedented housing boom. An ancillary wave of buying spiked demand for goods such as appliances, building materials, and furnishings. The demand for anything made in the United States was so high that competition emerged for labor and professional services. The concept of workers' rights, ignited by a new generation of eternal optimists, soon shifted the competitive nature of labor procurement to include Social Security–like pension benefits, health coverage, and onsite safety regulations, all worthy goals in and of themselves, particularly for a culture unconcerned about global competitiveness.

Not until the late 1960s did the economic juggernaut show the first signs of coming in for a landing. By this point, an entire generation had spent its formative years in a hall of plenty, shaping ideas and decisions for decades to come. Taking economic comfort as their birthright, the boomers dreamed. They dreamed of better lifestyles, and they dreamed of high-minded values of fairness, love, and cooperation. What they did not spend as much time dreaming about were the costs associated with such endeavors. Medicare, the original universal health care, as well as Social Security and corporate pension plans were questioned only by the staunchest conservatives. Their concerns were largely swept aside by a generation that had never felt pangs of hunger, and after all, given the life expectancy of the era, many boomers never expected to live long enough to collect meaningful benefits. So what could possibly go wrong?

Twenty-plus years in the making, the ensuing postwar cyclical expansion unwound for most of the 1970s. Housing, commercial real estate, and manufactured goods and commodities, all overpriced and overproduced as if demand would continue indefinitely, suddenly found no buyers. The period of unrest that followed proved pivotal in many ways. American workers, already the highest paid in the world and among the first to feel the pinch of reality, responded in a manner only possible for those accustomed to cornucopia: by demanding higher pay for less work. The theory had at its base the notion that if we could only keep out foreign competitors, business might continue as usual. Ignoring the reality that global trade had indeed fueled much of the economic growth of the previous two decades, trade barriers were erected, further exacerbating our economic woes.

The blame, however, did not rest solely on the shoulders of the U.S. labor force. Business leaders and the government were both quick to step in. Industry, feeling the squeeze by labor and anemic consumers, responded in two basic ways. First, to appease their workers, companies promised increased pension benefits, inadvertently kicking the can of responsibility further down the road; after all, the actuary tables of the day indicated that few workers would live long enough to collect the promised benefits. In addition, upon noticing that Japanese and other foreign manufacturers were actually gaining ground by producing what most considered low-quality goods, the captains of industry concluded that they should join the race for the bottom, cutting back on both the quantity and the quality of their raw materials. Our proverbial canary gasped for breath once again.

Unfortunately, while our industries were reducing the integrity of output, our competitors were determined to improve their efforts. In true American-centric fashion, only possible from those whose formative years knew no real competition, we waved flags and ignored the impending reality.

The American experience during this new age of idealism was in no way void of worry. Boomers lay awake at night assaulted by all sorts of worries, ranging from human rights and the state of the world to their own individual day-to-day machinations. While the concerns of their conscious existence were worldly in a way grander than perhaps those of any previous culture, subconsciously they remained naïve. This generation had spent its formative years, those that form who we are deep inside, which are generally solidified by the fifth year of life, largely isolated from the experience of hunger and bodily harm that had previously characterized so much of human existence. This base experience, as is typically the case, rarely emerged as a topic of discussion or subject of journalistic intrigue; rather it influenced our emotions, thus driving the behavior and experience of this one-of-a-kind slice of humanity. By the turn of the new century, the push and pull between conscious idealism and a recognition that we actually do live in a world with hunger, foreign threats, and other scary things would surface as the primary challenge of our nation.

John F. Kennedy, with true "greatest generation" valor, once urged our citizens to act responsibly. Unfortunately, this signaled the end, rather than a beginning, of this brand of responsible-minded politics. Soon, crafty candidates learned that if they promised voters "free" stuff, without a requirement to pay, the hollowness of the endeavor would go largely unnoticed. In succession, we witnessed the potentially cataclysmic overthrow of the long-held gold standard for our currency; the creation of a Social Security Commission charged with addressing the recent trend of unexpectedly long life spans (no sooner had the commission completed its work than politicians raided the funds); the demise of the traditional pension plan (unlike the government, corporations could not simply raise taxes to address the rapidly increasing lifespan and therefore created the 401k as a new option); the decline in the household savings rate, which peaked in the mid-1970s at over 14% of household income plummeted to −0.8% in the early part of the new century[19] (highlighting the difference between the behavior of the "greatest generation" during their peak earning years and that of the boomers during their heyday); and the crash of a strong housing market, which, for a host of reasons, turned into the debacle of a lifetime.

These are but a few examples of the interplay of godlike idealism set in a backdrop of a "can't lose" psyche. The notion of asking voters for any form of personal sacrifice wasn't considered seriously by either political party. By century's end, the only notable difference between these two behemoth organizations was what free stuff they promised and to whom. Perhaps a key question to ask is, why did we continue to vote for them? Again, one plausible explanation is the coupling of idealistic dreaming with a naïve formative experience.

In the first decade of this century we have lived through the unwinding of a tech-driven stock market bubble (the frenzied building of which was perhaps the first indication that panic stared back through the mirror at middle-aged boomers), the herd-like consumption of everything real estate and the resulting shockwave collapse of our economy, the near ruin of the world banking and finance system, a public safety net stretched beyond the tearing point, and a universal replacement of the traditional pension with the do-it-yourself 401k. So what do we do?

While volumes could be written outlining the entire scope of likely courses of action, the purpose of this work is to help the reader accept, and indeed embrace, individual responsibility as it relates to personal retirement planning efforts, the ramifications of which may be far greater than most imagine. Like it or not, we are a generation caught in transition. For decades, our leaders have promised benefits while simultaneously kicking the can of responsibility down the road. We find ourselves caring for aging parents while attempting to pay college tuition for our kids. Instead of relying on pension incomes, we now have to make choices about what to do with our 401k investments, and the once-stalwart Social Security system now looms as an unbearable burden on the shoulders of our children.

Rather than continuing to point the finger of blame, as *children* are so often apt to do, it is time we accept that government, business, and personal choice have all played a role in the creation of the current state of affairs. While few of us are in a position to change the status quo in Washington or single-handedly cause U.S. business leaders to adopt an outlook more meaningful than their quarterly bonus formula, we can all make better *personal* choices. The forced transition from a society of benefit recipients (pension and Social Security) to one of active asset owners (401k and IRA) offers both good and bad news. The good news is that we as a culture are on the verge of the greatest accumulation of wealth, and its subsequent generational transfer, that the world has ever witnessed. Average workers, diligently saving in a company retirement plan and then carefully making responsible retirement choices, will likely not only provide for their own comfort in old age but also potentially leave behind a nest egg for their children and grandchildren. The bad news is that for those who do not embrace this challenge, the safety nets are going away; a retirement lifestyle remotely resembling that of one's parents will seem unlikely indeed. In order to make the best possible retirement saving and planning decisions, we must begin by fully understanding the challenge at hand.

16

A Look Ahead

WHILE IT MAY be true that our recent historical choices (as a society) have occurred within the context of a subliminal backdrop in which less-than-responsible decision making emerged as a norm, it does not necessarily hold that our national journey must continue on a course inevitably leading to a third-world-like economic reality. From its beginning, the westernization of the Americas was forged from a raw material of personal responsibility. Imagine the courage needed to leave all that one knows and set out in a leaky boat for an unknown world. Whether braving the open seas for religious, political, or economic reasons, our forefathers boldly shaped their own destinies—destinies in which there were no guarantees and no safety nets. Our ancestors realized that an overreliance on safety nets left them at the whim of those who controlled the backstop. This is the stuff from which our nation was founded.

Hundreds of years later, the October 2009 issue of a well-known magazine featured a cover story calling for the death of the 401k. In this errant piece, the 401k was contrasted with the traditional pension, and it was suggested that the nation should move back to this safer and more guaranteed source of retirement income. While as a financial planner I can attest firsthand to the unparalleled degree to which a steady stream of income does in fact improve the stability of a financial planning scenario, the story and the mindset it reflects overlook an inescapable truth. The simple fact is, as mentioned previously in this book, the increase in human longevity has rendered these programs (including Social Security) difficult or impossible to manage in a cost-effective manner.

As appealing as the notion of a guaranteed retirement is, the reality for most is that we will increasingly be *required* to rely upon our own saving and investing efforts. This reality emerges not because anyone in particular wants the outcome, but because we are stuck with it. There can be no doubt that personal investment mistakes will be made, certain time periods will prove challenging, and a resulting vigilance will be required. **Those who choose to spend their energy longing for the mythical safety of a bygone era, or who fail to find their way to thorough and competent planning strategies, are likely to find a very harsh reality waiting at the end of their rainbow.** However, this seemingly bad news may prove to have a silver lining.

The widespread use of 401k and 403b retirement plans, and the forced discipline of automatic contributions which are so integral to these programs, can, when executed properly, shift an enormous amount of wealth into the hands of the average rank-and-file worker.

The shift in ownership of responsibility *from* government and industry *to* the shoulders of the average worker is both the good news and the bad news. You see, along with the shift in ownership of the responsibility comes a shift in the ownership of the assets.

—John Hauserman CFP®

For previous generations, retirement planning involved working for an employer for thirty or so years, retiring with a monthly stipend, and dying a few short years later. There were generally little more than token savings left behind to supplement an inheritance which otherwise amounted to no more than the family home. For workers who could not afford to own a home or who required long-term nursing care, there was typically nothing left for the kids. Looking to the future, however, we see a very different possibility emerging.

A worker who accepts the challenge of personal responsibility, builds a well-thought-out long-term strategy, and invests accordingly may expect to build a significant amount of wealth. These assets can be used for retirement income, and may also provide an inheritance and legacy for families which might otherwise be destined to toil in perpetual financial want. Consider the following hypothetical example:

A couple who earns $50,000 a year, diligently saves 6% of their paycheck, have employers who match the contribution, work for thirty years, and experience 8% growth on their pre-retirement savings could expect to accumulate about $1.25 million, not including any fees, charges, expenses, taxes, etc. and not taking into consideration inflation and market fluctuation. From that sum, after accounting for inflation, they could expect to draw the equivalent of $29,000 annually, thereby replacing approximately 60% of their income while leaving an inheritance of about $500,000 to their child (assuming a 5% rate of post-retirement investment return and 3% inflation).

Now, let's further assume that the child also labors under the exact same set of conditions, never earning more than $50,000 and retiring at about the same time that the diligent parents pass away. The child would reach retirement with just under $2 million from the 401k assets alone!

In this example it is important to note that the rates of return utilized are in keeping with historical market-based *average* returns. Obviously, your own circumstances might warrant different assumptions. It is also critical to note that the above assumptions do not support or imply any trading strategy or additional risk taking other than the maintenance of a well-diversified, asset-allocated, age-based portfolio approach. In other words, no fancy *market-beating* strategy was needed to achieve the sample results. The above does assume, however, that the investor was able to exercise sufficient wisdom and thereby avoid common behavioral mistakes.

At this point let's consider the following regulatory required disclosure:

> **Diversification, asset allocation, and systematic investment programs do not assure a profit or protect against losses in declining markets and cannot guarantee that any objective or goal will be achieved. Systematic investment programs involve continuous investment regardless of market conditions. Markets will fluctuate, and participants must consider their ability to continue investing during periods of low price levels.**

I hope the previous statement would go without saying for anyone who has made it thus far in this text. If it was not already made clear enough; there is no substitute for a well thought out systematic approach to financial planning which seeks to identify and comprehend the possible rewards and risks involved in any course of action.

In perhaps the ultimate income redistribution arrangement, widespread active participation in systematic investment programs like the 401k embody the potential to accumulate meaningful equity ownership in the hands of those most responsible of decision makers. This brings us to an important caveat: What exactly are the macroeconomic ramifications of millions of Americans accumulating many shares of stocks and stock-based mutual funds in their retirement plans? While it is true that this scenario exemplifies the importance for careful planning and improved decision making, there is perhaps a more significant implication to our economy as a whole.

Remembering our previous discussion regarding the factors necessary to create economic activity, you may recall that two of the essential elements include entrepreneurial risk taking coupled with the investment capital needed to turn vision into brick-and-mortar reality. The wave of cash which will likely become available with widespread 401k participation may very well provide the spark which ignites the next epic era of economic expansion. The investment dollars which are looking for a suitable home, in this example 401k contributions, may well provide the seed capital for future business operations.

In addition, the resulting accumulation of massive shares of domestic stock in the portfolios of the middle class has the potential to redirect corporate profits into the hands of the average citizen, thereby aligning the interests of business and the working class in a way never before experienced. This reality may in fact help bring about the end of the class warfare perpetuated largely by those who seek political or financial gain by harvesting its grim effects. Perhaps one of the harshest truths of all rests in the historical reality that class warfare at best merely shifts wealth from one group to another, but most often simply leaves those who lack resources further disenfranchised. In fact, my experience as a financial advisor indicates quite clearly that the surest way to align the interests of workers with their employer is to vest the rank-and-file in shares of company stock. Further, the more significant the employee ownership, the faster and more complete is the marriage of interests. While it is not my contention that employees should overload their portfolios with their employer's stock—diversification is essential—the alignment of interests to which I refer goes beyond that. In this scenario the interests of business and the middle class converge on a cultural level and will require more openness on the part of the business community combined with a more disciplined understanding on the part of the average worker. However, merely aligning the mindsets of average folks and corporate leadership is not the only potential benefit of the new retirement reality.

As Americans come to accept the critical and inevitable role that investing will have in their lives, they may develop a new wisdom. You see, the emotionally vested investor becomes a smarter shareholder. This is not to suggest that everyone needs to be able to analyze a corporate balance sheet or calculate the sharp ratio of their favorite mutual fund, merely that as the barriers between *us* and *them* collapse, responsible people may tend to analyze the headlines in a far more thoughtful manner. In so doing we may from a cultural standpoint find ourselves in a better position to cast our votes for those candidates, regardless of party affiliation, who *facilitate* personal and governmental responsibility rather than *hamper* it. We also may well find ourselves in a better position to cast our economic votes when we choose consumer products, select stocks, and vote our shares for corporate boards. In truth, if politicians recklessly promise *free stuff* in exchange for votes, we can remove them from office, and should we discover that the executives who are running a company in which we happen to own stocks have given themselves unwarranted lucrative bonuses, then we can jettison those shares driving down the value of the corporation. Additionally, involved shareholders do get a limited say in how a corporation is run by voting in person or by proxy at the annual shareholders meeting. Issues as critical as executive compensation and board membership are often decided at these mandated events. Such a simple solution requires no massive government body, no army of pensioned bureaucrats, and no special-interest-laden legislation, merely a flow of knowledge which provides investors with pertinent information germane to those organizations in which they are vested.

It is largely believed that with the manufacturing pressures posed by emerging economies, the way forward for the U.S. will be through creativity and innovation. There are two plausible outlets for this energy: services provided within the U.S. and problem-solving products and solutions geared for the rest of the world. A massive quantity of 401k-sponsored investment capital in search of a good home is exceptionally well suited for our domestic service industries. Most of those jobs, unlike manufacturing, *must* be performed domestically and therefore they remain resistant to foreign outsourcing. However, while it could be said that these services are by definition domestic, the same does not necessarily hold for the *profits* from those corporate concerns. In fact, the profits flow to shareholders who, with a nationally improved savings rate, could increasingly be American 401k participants and less often foreign interests.

While the U.S. is likely to continue to innovate in the realm of science, technology, and products which meet the demands of a growing world population (and increasing middle class), it is also likely that domestic manufacturing related to those endeavors will continue to escape overseas. It is that reallocation of world production which is responsible for the creation of a consuming middle class in those regions which were previously barren economically. Over the next two decades it is believed that the emerging market economies will create up to 700 million new entrants into the middle class, a figure roughly ten times the size of the boomer generation.[20] **This combination of a worldwide burgeoning middle class,**

free market contagion, and a newfound regional consumerism will promote an appetite for investment capital, much akin to that of the Industrial Revolution. What is different in this incarnation, however, is that today the capital (and future profits thereof) might be provided by the average American investor instead of a small number of overly wealthy tycoons. Therefore, while it may or may not be possible for the U.S. to regain its position as the singularly dominant *manufacturer* of world goods, it is entirely plausible that the American public, through a responsible savings rate, could own a significant share of the *profits* from international manufacturing. With this in mind it becomes clear that while the price of failure is unfathomably grave for boomers and their children, there also is nearly unlimited opportunity for a wealthy nation which acts responsibly, individuals who plan wisely, and corporations imbued with forward-looking leadership.

Notes

1   Dalbar, Inc., study on Quantitative Analysis of Investor Behavior (QAIB), updated 2009.
2   401k plans are generally subject to market volatility not typically found in whole life policies.
3   Author's opinion.
4   Morningstar Direct.
5   Not all stocks will pay dividends.
6   The formula used for the rule of 72 is used for approximating the time it will take for a given amount of money to double at a given compound interest rate. Compound illustrations are not predictions of investment performance, and investment principal and interest are not guaranteed and are subject to market fluctuation.
7   Morningstar Direct.
8   Morningstar Direct, 2010.
9   Author's opinion.
10 Author's opinion.
11 Ibbotson Associates.

12 Vehicle sales from *USA Today*, January 6, 2010; scrap rates from R.L. Polk & Co (www.polk.com).

13 U.S. Census Report by Jarmin and Miranda, 2007; "small and midsized businesses" are defined as those employing 1,000 or fewer workers.

14 Social Security Administration Trustees Report, 2008 (www.ssa.gov).

15 Social Security Administration Trustees Report, 2008 (www.ssa.gov).

16 U.S. Bureau of Economic Analysis (Department of Commerce).

17 U.S. Bureau of Economic Analysis (Department of Commerce).

18 Past performance does not guarantee future results.

19 U.S. Bureau of Economic Analysis (Department of Commerce).

20 Wharton School of Business, Knowledge@wharton, July 9, 2008.

*Nothing in this book should be construed as specific investment advice for any individual or as an offer or solicitation of any kind. This material is not intended for residents of all states due to regulatory and registration requirements regarding investment products and services. **Please visit** RetirementQuestWealthManagement.com **to** determine if John Hauserman is registered in your state. Individuals should seek out financial advice from qualified professionals familiar with their financial circumstances and then make their own financial decisions based upon such advice.*

Securities and advisory services offered through Commonwealth Financial Network (Commonwealth), member www.finra.org and www.sipc.org, a Registered Investment Adviser. Commonwealth and the above entities are separate and unrelated. Commonwealth does not offer tax or legal advice.

Index

401k
assets, 116
capital, providing, 96
defined benefit pension not
applicable, 14
equity investing and ownership,
65, 117
importance, 32–33
investment capital, 120
unexpected longevity, as
response to, 110
market volatility, 122n2
net worth security, 39
overconcentration, 47
pensions, replacing, 111
profiting, 34
seed capital, providing, 118
subtracting from gross, 9
value *vs.* whole life insurance, 41
wealth shifting, 114
withdrawals, 17–18
403b investment program, 32, 65,
114

A

account rebalancing, 53–56, 58–59
assets
accumulating with age, 39
active asset owners, 111, 115
asset allocation, 44–46, 54,
58–59, 116–117
below value, 76
cash, 64, 67
compiling for financial plan, 12
above the efficient frontier, 53
equity ownership, 65, 67
fee-only financial planners, 83
of guarantors, 61
vs. income portion of retirement
plan, 8
mutual fund purchases, 49

B

baby boomers
old assumptions, 4
greatest generation, contrasted
to, 110

naïveté, 105, 109
price of failure, 121
prosperous background, 106–107
as sandwich generation, 5
Social Security, inducing
shortfalls in, 70
war experiences, 103–105
back testing, 28–29
benefits
annual statement checks, 13
death, 37–41
defined benefit pension, 14
insurance policies, 37, 42
pension, 107, 108, 111
prescription drug, 97
promised to voters, 94
bonds
call features, 52, 63–64
creditworthiness, 62
dumping, 57
income guarantees, 65, 67
investments, 66–67
mutual fund purchases, 49
portfolios, 51, 55–56
price swings, 75
rebalancing, 54–55
web resource, 22
brokers
captive funds, 83–84
client funds, 76
client miscalculation, 44
discount, 80–82
encouraging sales, 53–54,
77–78
Bush, George W., 94

C

call features, 52, 63–64
capital gains, 66
captive funds, 83–84
cash
401k availability, 118
assets, 64
guarantee backing, 60–61, 65,
66–67
US trust fund comparison, 70
whole life insurance, 40–41
CDs, 50–51, 61
class warfare, 118
college, 3, 4–5, 8, 11
commodities, 65, 75, 107–108
convertible clause, 64
coupon rate, 62
credit
cards, 9, 14
political, 93
risk, 52, 62–63, 64
worthiness, 62

D

death benefits, 37–42
debts, 10, 14, 61–62, 66, 67, 94
dependents, 7, 10
discipline
account rebalancing, 55
equity investing, 66
of financial advisors, 84
financial planning, 57
portfolio investments, 35
savings, 4, 32, 33, 114
temptations to abandon, 68, 73

disclosures, required, 22–23, 45, 52, 116–117
discount brokers, 80–82
diversification, 47–49, 61, 116–117, 118
dollar-cost averaging, 33–35
dot-com era
  back-testing example, 29
  bursting of the tech bubble, 44, 74, 110
  Bush blamed for collapse, 94
  efficient frontier, 53
  investor mania, 49, 73, 78, 79–80
  learning from, 84
  portfolio risks, 42
  risk tolerance, 43

E

early retirement, 5, 13, 29, 79
efficient frontier, 45–46, 53, 56
equity, 14, 32–32, 65–67, 87–88, 117
estate planning, 10–11, 15, 42
estate taxes, 31

F

FICA, 8–9
financial advisors. *See also* brokers; Monte Carlo
  assessing, 16
  basic considerations, 6
  fee-only, 81, 83, 125
  financial salesmen, 56–57, 58
  guidelines on choosing, 83–84
  impact determination, 13, 37
  investor education, 76

investor fears, 74–75
  on life insurance policies, 39
  multiple scenarios, anticipating, 20
  overabundance, 30
  questioning, 24
  Registered Investment Advisor firms, 77, 82
  on risk, 25, 43, 44, 50
  types, 80, 81
  unfamiliar terms, helping with, 14
financial goals
  asset allocation, 45
  estate planning, 10–11
  financial planning, 92
  goal-setting, 6–7, 11
  likelihood of meeting, 30
  long term, 53, 66, 68, 76
  Monte Carlo analysis, 20
  options, 31–32
  reconsidering, 24
Financial Industry Regulatory Authority (FINRA), 22–23
financial planners. *See* financial advisors
financial plans
  continuous review, 20
  do-it-yourself investors, 85
  personal inventory, 12
  preparation, 97–98
  questioning workable outcomes, 35
  reducing risk/uncertainty, 92
  stability, 114
  viability, 10

fluctuations, 50, 61, 72, 87, 117,
        122n6
fraud, 76–77

G
goals. *See* financial goals
great recession, 61, 87–88, 92
gross income, 8–9

H
historical data
    back testing, 28–29
    on equity investments, 31–32, 67
    Monte Carlo simulations, 21–22
    risk and return assumptions,
        24–25
    stock market swings, 88
Hitler, Adolph, 100
housing
    boom, 106–107
    home equity loans, 14
    home ownership, 65
    homes as inheritance, 3, 115
    housing market crash, 110
    overextended homeowners, 91
    slow rate of home sales, 93

I
identity theft, 13
inflation
    accounting for, 50, 67, 72, 116
    assumptions, 18, 31
    planning for, 5, 11, 17
inheritances
    financially savvy parents, 50–51,
        116

overabundance, 30
personal responsibility, 112
in previous generations, 3–4, 115
remainder estate, 15
winner syndrome, 48
insurance. *See under* risk
        management
interest
    bonds, 52, 62–64
    cash investments, 61
    CDs, 50–51
    investment income, 8
    payoff date calculation, 14
    rule of 72, role in, 122n6
    in total return, 72
    whole life insurance policies, 40
investments. *See also* rate of return;
        risk management
    401ks, 32, 34, 111
    account rebalancing, 53–56
    account statements, 14
    asset allocation, 44–45
    back-testing, 28–29
    bond category, 61–64
    captive funds, 83–84
    cash category, 60–61
    dangerous goals, 6
    diversification, 28, 47–48, 50
    do-it-yourself investors, 82, 85
    emotional vestment, 119
    equity category, 65–68
    estate planning, 10–11
    financial services industry,
        history of, 77
    FINRA disclosure, 22–23
    fluctuations, 35

income drawn from, 51
inflation, adjusting for, 5
investment capital, 95, 96, 118, 120–121
life insurance policies, 40–42
Monte Carlo method, 20, 27, 33
mutual funds, 49
negative returns, 69
prediction difficulties, 24
responsible investing, 79–81
returns before Social Security, 3–4
rule of 72, 71, 122n6
services industry, 81–82
subtracting from gross, 8
swings, 87
systematic investment programs, 117
investor mistakes
avoidance, 116
common errors, 72
discount brokers, 81
failure to save, 33
fear-based, 74–76, 88–90
fundamentals, not understanding as cause, 16
as inevitable, 114
during market growth, 90–91
market timing, 92
market-savvy, benefiting, 86
oversimplified assumptions, 20
primal urges, blaming, 73
risk tolerance assessments, 44
temptations, giving into, 56–57, 67–68
vulnerability, due to, 78

J
Japanese goods, 106, 108
job growth, 95–96

K
Kennedy, John F., 109

L
life expectancy
financial forecast assumptions, 17–18
insurance policy rates, 40
prior expectations, exceeding, 3–5, 110
retirement planning, impact on, 7, 11
safety nets in danger, 69, 114

M
Medicare, 8, 94, 96–97, 107
middle class, 97, 118–119, 120–121
money-market funds, 60–61
Monte Carlo, 20–21, 23–24, 25, 27, 32, 33
mortgages, 4, 8–9, 10, 14, 89
mutual funds
cash investments, 60
customer service, 44
diversification, 49
dollar-cost averaging, 33
investor education, 119
investor sentiment, 73
macroeconomic ramifications, 117
Monte Carlo method, 23
motto, 82

outflow, 90
web resource, 22

N

negative returns, 55–56, 69
number crunching, 16–17, 30
nursing-homes, 3–4, 11, 115

O

overabundance, 30–31, 35

P

payroll-deducted strategy. *See* 401k
pension plans
  401ks and, 111, 114
  benefits increase, 108
  corporate, 107
  demise of, 110
  longevity affecting, 17, 69
  old assumptions, 4
  statements, 13–14
portfolios
  account rebalancing, 53–59
  asset allocation, 44–46
  diversification, 47–49, 50–51, 61,
    66, 116, 118
  dot-com bubble, 80
  fluctuations in investment
    markets, 33, 35
  higher than average returns, 24
  hypothetical example, 67
  inflation affecting, 18, 71
  Monte Carlo simulations, 20–22,
    25, 33
  overabundance, 30
  rate of return, 31–32

risk tolerance, 42
rule of 72, 71–72
types, 26–28
prescription drug coverage, 97

R

rate of return. *See also* investments
  account rebalancing, 55
  crunching the numbers, 17
  equity ownership, 66
  expectations, 18
  fluctuations, 19–21
  goal setting, 6
  growth periods, 90
  historical averages, 67, 116
  historically based assumptions,
    22, 24
  investor mistakes, 57
  Monte Carlo simulations, 21, 23,
    25
  negative returns, 69
  portfolio altering, 31–32
  portfolio types, 26–28
  risk-return relationship, 45–46
  rule of 72, 71–72
  unlikely numbers, 80
  volatility, 33–35
  of yesteryear, 3–4
real estate, 53, 65, 73, 107, 110
rebalancing, 53–56, 58–59
remainder estate, 15
required disclosures, 22–23, 45, 52,
  116–117
RetirementQuest website
  Distribution City stop, 10, 14
  Final Destination section, 15

planning map, 16–17, 125, 126
state registration check, 124
Tax Law Quagmire selection, 31
Tool Box link, 10, 22, 70
risk management. *See also*
portfolios; rate of return
account rebalancing, 53–55
addressed in thorough planning, 11
back-testing, 28
bonds, 52, 62, 63–64
CDs, 50
entrepreneurial risk taking, 94, 95–96, 117–118
equities as risky, 66
financial planning reducing risk, 80, 92
insurance
disability protection, 36–37
guarantees, 60–61
motto, 82
selling culture, 77
term, 37–39
universal life, 37, 39, 42
whole life, 37, 39–42
low volatility risks, 26
middlemen, 61
Monte Carlo results, 23, 25
overconcentration, 47, 49
parameters, 6
risk tolerance, 42–44, 53, 55, 72
short-term risks, 32, 45, 46, 67
widely accepted assumptions, 24
rule of 72, 71–72, 122n6

S
Saturday dilemma, 7–8
savings
through 401ks, 32–33
average workers, 111
cash investments, 67
disciplined approach, 32
exhausting, 50
longevity as factor, 5
Medicare, 96
nationally improved rate, 120
not saving enough, 66
profit sharing, 121
rate declines, 102, 110
relying on, 114
statements, 14
subtracting from gross, 8
universal life insurance, 42
vehicles of, 60
of yesteryear, 4, 115
Security Investors Protections Corporation (SIPC), 77
Social Security
anticipation of changes, 11, 70–71
baby boomers, 107
beginnings, 3–4
benefit formula, alteration, 12
benefit statements, checking, 13
longevity as factor, 17, 69, 109–110, 114
societal changes, 111
subtracting from gross, 8
taxes, 70, 94
Stalin, Joseph, 99, 100
standard deviation, 23, 25

stock market
dollar-cost averaging, 33–35
dot-com era, 43–44, 110
investor error, 57–58, 73–76
market cycle vacillations, 53, 86–88
market timing, 92
politics, role of, 91, 93–94
recovery, 90
whole life insurance policies, 40
stocks
account rebalancing, 53–57
convertible clause, 64
defined, 66
diversified investing, 47, 65
dividends, 122n5
dot-com era, 78
factors driving prices, 75–76
investor emotion, 88–90
involved shareholders, 119
macroeconomic ramifications, 117–118
Monte Carlo method, 23
in portfolios, 28, 31
primal urges, 73
short-term risks, 67
technology, 43
web resource, 22
subtract from gross method, 8–9

T

taxes
401ks, 41, 65, 110

items extinguished after retirement, 8–9
payroll, 70
property, 10
raising to cover deficit, 94–95
role in economic growth, 96
taking into account, 50, 67, 72
tax efficiency, 31

V

volatility
401k plans subject to, 122
bonds, 52, 55–56, 64
equity holdings, 31–32
illustrations, 51
investor account balances, 88
low risk as failing strategy, 26
Monte Carlo and portfolios, 20–21, 33
short-term, 45–46

W

winner syndrome, 48–49
withdrawals
from 401k plans, 17
for annual incomes, 18, 35
back-testing, 28
cutting back on, 10
from investment accounts, 19
Monte Carlo analysis, 21, 25

Y

younger workers, 32, 35, 38–39, 40–42, 67

John Hauserman, CFP®

John is a CERTIFIED FINANCIAL PLANNER™ practitioner, creator of the RetirementQuest® interactive planning map, and frequent guest financial expert on several television news broadcasts. With nearly twenty years of advising experience, and as an Investment Advisor Representative of Commonwealth Financial Network, he has helped individuals meet their financial goals and has championed fee-only financial planning as a fairer and more conflict-free method to deliver financial services. John created RetirementQuest® and authored this book, out of his deep concern for the financial well-being of the investing public. This book is one part of his unending commitment to help Americans rise to the challenge that is the financial planning process.

John conducts his financial practice at his offices in suburban Baltimore, 2600 Longstone Lane, Suite 105, Marriottville, Maryland 21104. For more information, please visit www.RetirementQuestWealthManagement.com or call 877-233-4912. Securities and advisory services offered through Commonwealth Financial Network®, member www.finra.org and www.sipc.org, a Registered Investment Adviser.

Away from work, John enjoys time with his wife, Diane, and children, Jackson and Leah. Together they share a love of music, sports, travel, and outdoor activities.

About the RetirementQuest®

Interactive Planning Map

The no-cost interactive planning map was designed to help site users (www.RetirementQuest.com) gain a more thorough understanding of the financial planning process in the comfort of their own homes and at the leisure of their own pace. Laid out in a format that most users find easy to understand, the map enables individuals to drill as deep or remain as cursory as their level of financial literacy warrants. While the map is not designed to replace financial planning software or personal advisors, it is intended to help users evaluate and improve the competency of their current sources of advice or ability to function as a do-it-yourself planner. RetirementQuest.com and the interactive planning map are intended for educational use only. Those seeking a personal financial advisor may wish to visit www.RetirementQuestWealthManagement.com or call the author at 877-233-4912.